THE LINCOLN-DOUGLAS DEBATES

DOVER THRIFT EDITIONS

Abraham Lincoln and Stephen A. Douglas

Edited by Edwin Erle Sparks

DOVER PUBLICATIONS, INC.
MINEOLA, NEW YORK

DOVER THRIFT EDITIONS

GENERAL EDITOR: SUSAN L. RATTINER
EDITOR OF THIS VOLUME: STEPHANIE CASTILLO SAMOY

Bibliographical Note

This Dover edition, first published in 2018, is an unabridged republication of the work originally printed in 1918 by F. A. Owen Publishing Company, Dansville, New York. A new introductory note has been specially prepared for this volume.

Library of Congress Cataloging-in-Publication Data

Names: Lincoln, Abraham, 1809–1865, author. | Douglas, Stephen A. (Stephen Arnold), 1813–1861, author. | Sparks, Edwin Erle, 1860–1924, editor.
Title: The Lincoln-Douglas debates / Abraham Lincoln and Stephen A. Douglas ; edited by Edwin Erle Sparks.
Description: Mineola, New York : Dover Publications, 2018. | Series: Dover thrift editions | "Unabridged republication of the work originally published in 1918 by F. A. Owen Publishing Company, Dansville, New York"—Back of title page.
Identifiers: LCCN 2018001950| ISBN 9780486817231 (paperback) | ISBN 0486817237 (pbk)
Subjects: LCSH: Lincoln-Douglas Debates, Ill., 1858. | United States—Politics and government—1857–1861. | Lincoln, Abraham, 1809–1865—Political career before 1861. | BISAC: HISTORY / United States / Civil War Period (1850–1877). | LANGUAGE ARTS & DISCIPLINES / Rhetoric. | LANGUAGE ARTS & DISCIPLINES / Public Speaking. | POLITICAL SCIENCE / Political Process / Elections. | POLITICAL SCIENCE / General.
Classification: LCC E457.4 .L535 2018 | DDC 973.6/8092—dc23
LC record available at https://lccn.loc.gov/2018001950

Manufactured in the United States by LSC Communications
81723703   2020
www.doverpublications.com

Contents

NOTE

It was 1858—less than two hundred years ago—when two candidates went toe to toe for the opportunity to represent Illinois in the US Congress. One was six feet four inches, an attorney and a former state representative. The other was a foot shorter (maybe even more, according to some sources) and was the incumbent senator.

Abraham Lincoln, a member of the newly formed Republican Party, was a less seasoned and entrenched politician on the national scene than Stephen A. Douglas, who was known as "the Little Giant" because of his short stature yet forceful presence. Douglas was a favorite figure in the Democratic Party and gunning for the US presidency in the near future.

Douglas traveled by private train from town to town, campaigning for his reelection. Lincoln often immediately followed him, taking advantage of the huge crowds, and responded to folks' questions about his opponent's stances. Douglas finally agreed to add seven extra dates to his already full schedule so that the two men could appear in public together.

The results are in the history books: Lincoln won the popular vote, but Douglas won the legislative districts. Douglas was named US senator once again. However, the Lincoln-Douglas debates eventually catapulted the gangly gentleman, originally from Kentucky and Indiana, to the highest seat of government and to becoming one of the best-loved figures in US history.

INTRODUCTION

Stump Speaking—As the American people pushed their way across the continent from the Atlantic to the Pacific, the thin edge of advancing civilization was known as the "frontier." It was made up of courageous spirits who subdued the Indians, drove the French and Spanish from their pathway, slew the wild beasts, felled the forests, built their log cabins, and planted their fields. Daniel Boone and Davy Crockett belonged to these hardy people. Cut off from the comforts and privileges which they had enjoyed before migrating to "the West," these people resorted to various makeshifts to supply their needs. They used Indian moccasins on their feet, and coonskin caps on their heads. Lacking newspapers, they learned the issues of the political campaigns by assembling to hear the candidates who, in turn, mounted the stump of a felled tree in the streets of the frontier town and from that forum addressed the voters. A good "stump speaker" could always attract a crowd, and a wit combat between two speakers representing opposite parties was a real holiday of sport. It is true that the jokes and counter-strokes were often feeble attempts, and sometimes not very far removed from vulgarity; but the stronger the blows the better they were liked, and the more personal, the more enjoyable they were.

The spirit of democracy was strong in these pioneers and made them intensely interested in politics. Their fondness for hearing political speeches, their attendance upon political meetings, their parades, floats, banners, and bands remained even after the first frontier stage of progress had passed and the country was well settled. In Illinois, stump speaking was popular as late as 1858, although the frontier had passed on into Kansas and Nebraska, just ready for statehood.

Political Parties—The slavery question was always a festering thorn in the side of the body politic, frequently poulticed by compromises, but manifesting itself whenever a new national issue arose. The Abolitionists, headed by William Lloyd Garrison, Wendell Phillips, and others, opposed all compromises and stood for the unconditional and immediate emancipation of the slaves. They were bitterly condemned by both the Whig and Democrat parties as wild and dangerous reformers, who were likely to bring about a dissolution of the Union through their agitation. Each party denied any sympathy for or connection with the Abolitionists.

The contention of the Abolitionists that slavery was wrong ethically, made little progress until it became an economic and political matter through the proposed statehood for Kansas and Nebraska. The prairies were not fitted climatically for cotton raising, which made slaveholding profitable; but if two new States came in free, as they must do under the Compromise of 1820,[1] they would add four free Senators and many free Congressmen to the Northern strength, thereby further curbing the slaveholding power in national affairs.

The demand of the South for an adjustment led, in 1854, to the substitution for the Missouri Compromise of 1820 of a new remedy (the Kansas-Nebraska measure) which, by permitting the people of the proposed states to determine whether they would be free or slave, was thought to be the very essence of democracy or home rule. As usual, in temporizing with the evil the remedy became worse than the disease.

The Republican Party—This setting aside of the Missouri Compromise for "squatter sovereignty" banded together Northern Whigs and Northern Democrats on an anti-slavery platform; and they speedily formed a new party, calling themselves Republicans. In 1856 the new party had a candidate for

---

[1] The Missouri Compromise of 1820 provided that Missouri should come into the Union as a slave State, but that thereafter in the territory acquired by the Louisiana Purchase, slavery should be forever prohibited north of latitude 36° 30', which was the line of the southern boundary of Missouri.

the presidency, Fremont, and parties were now known polit-ically as Democrats, Old Line Whigs, and Republicans. The first two refused to recognize the Republican movement as more than a conspiracy or corrupt bargain between leaders to break up the old parties and bring themselves into political power. In the debates it will be noticed that Douglas assails the corrupt bargain between Lincoln, an Old Line Whig, and Trumbull, a Democrat, both of whom deserted the old parties to join the new Republican party.

The Little Giant—Stephen A. Douglas, a Senator from Illinois and a Northern Democrat, was chairman of the Senate Committee on Territories. As such he pushed the Kansas-Nebraska bill of 1854 through both Houses, and incurred the criticism of the free soil advocates of both parties in the North. He said later that he could have traveled from Washington to his home in Chicago, when Congress adjourned, by the light of himself being burned in effigy. For three hours in his home town he tried in vain to get his con-stituents to listen to his explanations.

Douglas was born in Vermont, migrated to Illinois, and had advanced rapidly through the offices of prosecuting attorney, State legislator, Registrar of Public Lands, candidate for Congress, State Supreme Court Judge, Congressman for two terms, and finally, in 1845, member of the United States Senate. He had served two terms in the Senate, and in 1858 was a candidate for a third election by the State legislature. He had a most winning personality, a fearless spirit, a quick temper, and an unlimited energy of physical force and will power. He was short and heavy in figure, but possessed a far-reaching voice, and early acquired the nickname of "The Little Giant." In stump speaking he was considered the champion of the Middle West.

Honest Old Abe—Among those who watched with interest the course of The Little Giant was Abraham Lincoln, a member of the Whig party, who wrote to a friend in 1854 that Douglas's action might have created an opening for a Whig Senator from Illinois, and "if so, I want the chance of being that man;" but it was thought best to nominate Lyman Trumbull. Four years later Lincoln had the opportunity.

Lincoln started even lower in life than Douglas, and progressed more slowly. He lacked Douglas's personal magnetism and suffered still more by comparison of appearance. He was tall, ungainly, and careless in his dress. He was also hampered all his life by poverty. On the other hand, he possessed more natural shrewdness than Douglas, and always kept his temper, even under the flings of Douglas. His habits of life were extremely temperate and formed a marked contrast to other men in public life at that time.

Lincoln and Douglas knew each other at the State Capital, and in the Courts where both practiced law. Lincoln had taken little part in politics except to serve a term in Congress, 1847–9. He was a candidate for the Senate in 1854, as has been said, but withdrew in favor of Trumbull. Small wonder that many thought him presumptuous in aspiring to the United States Senate in 1858, and especially when that meant to oppose the great Douglas. The task seemed doubly hard because Lincoln was the candidate of a new party, the Republican or "Black Republican," as the Democrats dubbed it because of its espousal of the rights of the negro.

Political Conditions—It was customary at that time to hold nominating conventions some months before elections. The State Legislatures elected the United States Senators, and so the choice of members of the Legislature in senatorial election years was a matter of vital importance. Illinois had always been Democratic, and Douglas felt no apprehension in the senatorial election of 1857 except so far as the Kansas-Nebraska turmoil should disturb normal conditions. Late in 1857 some of the residents of the Territory of Kansas had formed, at Lecompton, a pro-slavery constitution for the proposed State. President Buchanan favored the adoption of the "Lecompton Constitution," but Douglas opposed it on the ground that it was not a fair test of the theory of "squatter sovereignty;" all the people of the Territory had not taken part. The Democratic party in Illinois was therefore in a divided condition, and there might be some shifting to the new Republican party if it came out with a strong Free-Soil platform. The fears of the Democratic party leaders were realized, April 21, 1858, when the Democratic State Committee met at Springfield and nominated Douglas on an anti-Lecompton platform, which caused a number of the delegates to "bolt" the convention, and, six weeks later, to hold another convention and nominate another ticket.

Consequently, it was with high hopes that the new Republican party met in convention at Springfield in June, and resolved that Abraham Lincoln was the first and only choice of the Republicans of Illinois for the United States Senate as the successor of Stephen A. Douglas. The speech which Lincoln had prepared for the convention he read from manuscript, a thing which he rarely did, and he also carefully read the proof in the printing office before the speech was published. He was stating the principles of the new party and, as it chanced, of a new era in American politics. Douglas would make every use of the platform, and Lincoln must be careful to see that it was so plain that its statements could not be twisted or misconstrued by the wily debater.

The two strong factors in the campaign were the situation in the Kansas-Nebraska territory, and a recent decision by the Supreme Court of the United States. This held in the case of Dred Scott,[2] a fugitive slave, that no negro slave or his descendant can ever be a citizen of a State, that neither

---

[2] Dred Scott was a slave in Missouri, a slave State ; his owner took him in 1834 to Illinois, a free State; then, in 1834, to Minnesota, a free Territory. Later his owner took him back to Missouri, when he sued for his freedom, on the ground that he had resided, for a while at least, on free soil. His owner claimed that having been born of slave parentage and never having been set free, he was still a slave, notwithstanding his places of temporary residence. In 1857 the Supreme Court of the United States decided in favor of the owner.

Congress nor a State Legislature can exclude slavery from a
State or Territory, and that the decision whether a slave can
be held in a free State depends upon the courts of that State.
Douglas saw how inconsistent this decision was with his
squatter sovereignty theory, and was driven to say that he
"cared not whether slavery was voted up or voted down,"
provided the people had a fair vote on the question. Lincoln
in his speech at the Republican nominating convention
seized the opportunity to point out where the development
of events had put Douglas. "His friends," he said, "remind us
that he is a great man and that the largest of us are very small
ones. Let this be granted. But 'a living dog is better than a
dead lion.' Judge Douglas, if not a dead lion, for this work is
at least a caged and toothless one."

In opening the speech, Lincoln used a paraphrase of Mark
3:25 which was prophetic and destined to become immortal,
although Douglas later declared it seditious. Lincoln said:

"*Mr. President and Gentlemen of the Convention:* If we could
know where we are, and whither we are tending, we could
better judge what to do, and how to do it. We are now far
into the fifth year since a policy was initiated with the
avowed object and confident promise of putting an end to
slavery agitation. Under the operation of that policy, that
agitation has not only not ceased, but has constantly augmented. In my opinion, it will not cease until a crisis shall
have been reached and passed. 'A house divided against itself
cannot stand.' I believe this government cannot endure permanently half slave and half free. I do not expect the Union
to be dissolved; I do not expect the house to fall; but I do
expect it will cease to be divided. It will become all one
thing or all the other. Either the opponents of slavery will
arrest the further spread of it, and place it where the public
mind shall rest in the belief that it is in the course of ultimate
extinction, or its advocates will push it forward till it shall
become alike lawful in all the States, old as well as new,
North as well as South."

Such was the condition of affairs at the opening of the campaign between Douglas and Lincoln for the senatorship of Illinois in 1858.

The Challenge—Douglas at once gave out a list of his speaking appointments for July, and closing on August 21 at Ottawa. The Republicans also prepared a list of Republican meetings at which Lincoln was scheduled to speak, in some cases coinciding with the Democratic dates and in others following a day later. At the meetings the crowd sometimes called upon Lincoln to reply to Douglas and the Democratic papers complained that Lincoln was showing bad taste in following Douglas about and taking advantage of his large audiences. Douglas devoted a larger part of his time to Trumbull, his co-senator from Illinois, whom he accused of making a compact with Lincoln to dissolve both the old Whig and old Democratic parties and to unite with the Abolitionists in forming the new "Black" Republican party. Trumbull, in turn, charged Douglas with making a corrupt bargain in favoring the repeal of the Missouri Compromise measure.

It appeared as if the campaign would resolve itself into a contest between Douglas and Trumbull, while Lincoln, who was the actual candidate for Douglas's place, would be lost sight of. Consequently, after consulting his friends, Lincoln wrote to Douglas, July 24, 1858, inquiring whether it would be agreeable "to divide time and address the same audiences in the present canvass." Douglas replied the same day that his schedule had been made out, that the Democratic candidates for other offices on the State ticket must be given a hearing at his meetings; but that he would arrange seven extra meetings at which he would discuss the issues of the day with Lincoln. He further named the places, one in each of the seven Congressional districts of the State, omitting the Springfield and Chicago districts, in which both had already spoken through Lincoln's "follow-up" method.

Lincoln accepted the seven places and the following letters closed the arrangements:

Bement, Piatt Co., Ill., July 30, 1858

Dear Sir:——

Your letter dated yesterday, accepting my proposition for a joint discussion at one prominent point in each Congressional District, as stated in my previous letter, was received this morning.

The times and places designated are as follows:

Ottawa, LaSalle County   August 21,1858.
Freeport, Stephenson County   "   27,   "
Jonesboro, Union County   September 15,   "
Charleston, Coles County   "   18,   "
Galesburg, Knox County   October 7,   "
Quincy, Adams County   "   13,   "
Alton, Madison County   "   15,   "

I agree to your suggestion that we shall alternately open and close the discussion. I will speak at Ottawa for one hour, you can reply, occupying an hour and a half, and I will then follow for half an hour. At Freeport you shall open the discussion and speak for one hour. We will alternate in like manner in each successive place. Very respectfully, your obedient servant,

S. A. DOUGLAS

Hon. A. Lincoln, Springfield, Ill.

Springfield, July 31, 1858.

Hon. S. A. Douglas.

Dear Sir:

Yours of yesterday, naming places, times, and terms, for joint discussions between us, was received this morning. Although, by the terms, as you propose, you take *four* openings and closings, to my *three,* I accede, and thus close the arrangement. I direct this to you at Hillsboro and shall try to have both your letter and this appear in the *Journal* and *Register* of Monday morning.

Your obedient servant,
A. LINCOLN.

The newspapers of the State approved of this arrangement to "let the people judge for themselves who shall be their choice after a fair hearing of them both in person" and to "submit the whole case to such popular jurors, called together by the joint efforts of the two parties." The Douglas papers made flings at the egotism and the presumption of the upstart to try to thrust himself upon the public by using the crowds which would come to hear The Little Giant.

The Course of the Debates—The series began August 21 and closed October 15, covering a period of nearly eight weeks. Douglas began immediately an attack on the new Republican party, of which his opponent was one of the founders, and claimed that a bargain had been made between his former fellow Democrat, Judge Trumbull, and Abraham Lincoln, to unite with the Abolitionists in a sectional revolt against slavery; a course which would endanger the Union. He used Lincoln's "house divided against itself" as proof of this disloyalty. Lincoln denied the charge of Abolitionism and stated in simple language his opinion of the rights of the negro; and then opened up the record of Douglas on the territorial extension of slavery and the Dred Scott case.

It was customary for a debater to ask his opponent a series of questions intended to compromise him or to put him in an embarrassing position. Douglas did this in the very first debate, hoping to set a trap for Lincoln; but in the second debate Lincoln answered these questions and then countered with four sequential questions which some historians think caught Douglas in his own trap.

This second (Freeport) debate is considered the most important of the series. The second question of Lincoln, as to the right of a people of a Territory to exclude slavery before becoming a State, made Douglas reaffirm what he had said "a hundred times from every stump in Illinois." He had to choose between an affirmative answer, which would please Northern Democrats and gain him the Senatorship, but bar all hopes of the presidency through alienating the South; or returning a

negative answer, which would cost him his Northern favor
and the Senatorship. Also, an affirmative reply would be
wholly at variance with the Dred Scott decision. Nevertheless
he answered affirmatively.

It is said that Lincoln saw the result of the affirmative reply
which Douglas would probably give and which would cost
Lincoln the senatorship, but that he looked forward to the
presidential election of 1860, and in his homely vernacular
said, "I am after larger game." Admirers of Douglas doubt this
story, and deny that Lincoln drove Douglas into a corner,
because Douglas had on several prior occasions declared that
the people of a Territory can, by lawful means, exclude slavery
from their limits prior to the formation of a State Constitution.

In the next debate Douglas reiterated his "bargain" claim,
and expressed his unconcern whether slavery was "voted up or
voted down" in a Territorial legislature. This involved the idea
that matters should go on as they had been, but Lincoln
showed that Douglas by his own action had made this impossible. Lincoln also exploded Douglas' theory of squatter sovereignty by saying that it simply amounted to this: "That if any
one man choose to enslave another, no third man shall be
allowed to object." The compact with Trumbull and many
items of local Illinois politics were frequently tossed back and
forth between the two. These are omitted from this volume
because they had no bearing on the national situation.

At Jonesboro, Douglas took a fling at negroes mingling
with whites, and insinuated that Lincoln and the Republicans
were in favor of the equality of the two races. To this Lincoln
said the final word at Charleston in regard to the possibility
of a white man marrying a colored woman.

There were several passages at arms between the debaters,
and some crude banter which would scarcely be considered in
good taste at present. The least justifiable was Douglas reviving
the old falsehood that while in Congress in 1847 Lincoln had
voted against sending supplies to our troops fighting in Mexico.
Lincoln was manifestly aroused to anger, as his reply shows. But
he was even more angered when Douglas poked fun at him

about his powers of physical endurance, suggesting that Lincoln was so exhausted at Ottawa that he had to be carried from the platform, when in truth he had been carried away, despite his protests, on the shoulders of his enthusiastic followers.

Douglas frequently lost his temper when interrupted, as he was at Freeport by his hearers who took exception to his constant use of the term "Black" Republican. To his complaint that no Democrat had been vulgar and blackguard enough to interrupt Lincoln while he had the platform, Lincoln replied that while he was speaking he has used no vulgarity or blackguardism toward the Democrats in the crowd.

The Results of the Debates—Extracts from the debates were printed in the leading newspapers from New York to St. Louis. Douglas's "Freeport doctrine" was strongly denounced by the Southern people. It made him impossible to them as a candidate for the presidency in 1860 and this caused a split in the Democratic party and the election of Lincoln. Lincoln lost the senatorship, as his friends had predicted.[3] He borrowed enough money to pay all obligations incurred during the campaign, and expressed himself as satisfied because he had "got a hearing." Only two debates have come down by name in American history: one is the Hayne-Webster and the other is the Lincoln-Douglas. The former established the standing of the Constitution; the latter paved the way for the thirteenth, fourteenth, and fifteenth amendments.

---

[3] Lincoln received a majority of 4,085 in the popular vote. In spite of this, the arrangement of the Legislative districts, together with hold-over Senators, was such that the Democrats secured 14 seats in the Senate to 11 for the Republicans, and 40 in the House to 35 Republicans.

FIRST JOINT DEBATE

Ottawa, August 21, 1858

MR. DOUGLAS'S SPEECH

Ladies and Gentlemen: I appear before you to-day for the purpose of discussing the leading political topics which now agitate the public mind. By an arrangement between Mr. Lincoln and myself, we are present here to-day for the purpose of having a joint discussion, as the representatives of the two great political parties of the State and Union, upon the principles in issue between those parties; and this vast concourse of people shows the deep feeling which pervades the public mind in regard to the questions dividing us.

Prior to 1854 this country was divided into two great political parties, known as the Whig[4] and Democratic parties. Both were national and patriotic, advocating principles that were universal in their application. . . . The Whig party and the Democratic party jointly adopted the compromise measures of 1850[5] as the

---

[4] The Whig party arose about 1825, although the name was not used until some years later. Henry Clay, John Quincy Adams, and Daniel Webster were the great leaders. The Democratic party came into existence about the same time, under Andrew Jackson's leadership.

[5] The Compromise of 1850 involved the admission of California, the organization of New Mexico and Utah as territories, to be free or slave States as their inhabitants might decide (squatter sovereignty), the payment of a money indemnity to Texas, a more rigid Fugitive Slave law, and the abolition of the slave trade, but not of slavery, in the District of Columbia.

1

basis of a proper and just solution of this slavery question in all its forms.

Up to 1853–54, the Whig party and the Democratic party both stood on the same platform with regard to the slavery question. That platform was the right of the people of each State and each Territory to decide their local and domestic institutions for themselves, subject only to the Federal Constitution.

During the session of Congress of 1853–54, I introduced into the Senate of the United States a bill to organize the Territories of Kansas and Nebraska on that principle which had been adopted in the Compromise measures of 1850. . . . I put forth the true intent and meaning of the Act in these words: "It is the true intent and meaning of this Act not to legislate slavery into any State or Territory, or to exclude it therefrom, but to leave the people thereof perfectly free to form and regulate their domestic institutions in their own way, subject only to the Federal Constitution." Thus, you see, that up to 1854, when the Kansas and Nebraska bill was brought into Congress for the purpose of carrying out the principles which both parties had up to that time indorsed and approved, there had been no division in this country in regard to that principle except the opposition of the Abolitionists[6]. . . .

In 1854, Mr. Abraham Lincoln and Mr. Trumbull[7] entered into an arrangement, one with the other, and each with his respective friends, to dissolve the old Whig party on the one hand, and to dissolve the old Democratic party on the other, and to connect the members of both into an Abolition party, under the name and disguise of a Republican party. . . . Lincoln went to work to Abolitionize the old Whig party all over the State, pretending that he was then as good a Whig as ever; and Trumbull went to work in his part of the State

---

[6] The Abolitionists wished to free all slaves by an amendment to the Constitution, without compensation to the owners.

[7] Lyman Trumbull, lawyer, was born in Connecticut in 1813, settled in Illinois, and became Secretary of State of Illinois in 1841, Justice of the State Supreme Court in 1848, and U. S. Senator in 1855. He was a Democrat, but joined the new Republican party in 1855.

preaching Abolitionism in its milder and lighter form, and trying to Abolitionize the Democratic party, and bring old
Democrats handcuffed and bound hand and foot into the
Abolition camp. In pursuance of the arrangement, the parties
met at Springfield in October, 1854, and proclaimed their new
platform. . . . I have the resolutions of their State Convention
then held, which was the first mass State Convention ever held
in Illinois by the Black Republican party, and I now hold them
in my hands and will read a part of them, and cause the others
to be printed. Here are the most important and material resolutions of this Abolition platform:—

1. Resolved, That we believe this truth to be self-evident, that
   when parties become subversive of the ends for which they
   are established, or incapable of restoring the Government to
   the true principles of the Constitution, it is the right and duty
   of the people to dissolve the political bands by which they
   may have been connected therewith, and to organize new
   parties upon such principles and with such views as the circumstances and exigencies of the nation may demand.

2. Resolved, That the times imperatively demand the reorga-
   nization of parties, and, repudiating all previous party attach-
   ments, names, and predilections, we unite ourselves together
   in defense of the liberty and Constitution of the country, and
   will hereafter cooperate as the Republican party, pledged to
   the accomplishment of the following purposes: To bring the
   administration of the Government back to the control of first
   principles; to restore Nebraska and Kansas to the position of
   free Territories; that, as the Constitution of the United States
   vests in the States, and not in Congress, the power to legislate for the extradition of fugitives from labor, to repeal and
   entirely abrogate the Fugitive Slave Law;[8] to restrict slavery
   to those States in which it exists; to prohibit the admission
   of any more Slave States into the Union; to abolish slavery

---

[8] The Fugitive Slave law was part of the Compromise of 1850. It placed
the duty of returning runaway slaves in the hands of United States
Marshals. instead of State officers.

in the District of Columbia; to exclude slavery from all the Territories over which the General Government has exclusive jurisdiction; and to resist the acquirement of any more Territories unless the practice of slavery therein forever shall have been prohibited.

3. Resolved, That in furtherance of these principles we will use such Constitutional and lawful means as shall seem best adapted to their accomplishment, and that we will support no man for office, under the General or State Government, who is not positively and fully committed to the support of these principles, and whose personal character and conduct is not a guarantee that he is reliable, and who shall not have abjured old party allegiance and ties.[9]

Now, gentlemen, your Black Republicans have cheered every one of those propositions, and yet I venture to say that you cannot get Mr. Lincoln to come out and say that he is now in favor of each one of them. That these propositions, one and all, constitute the platform of the Black Republican party of this day, I have no doubt; and when you were not aware for what purpose I was reading them, your Black Republicans cheered them as good Black Republican doctrines. My object in reading these resolutions was to put the question to Abraham Lincoln this day, whether he now stands and will stand by each article in that creed and carry it out. I desire to know whether Mr. Lincoln to-day stands, as he did in 1854, in favor of the unconditional repeal of the Fugitive Slave law. I desire him to answer whether he stands pledged to-day, as he did in 1854, against the admission of any more Slave States into the Union, even if the people want them. I want to know whether he stands pledged against the admission of a new State into the Union with such a Constitution as the people of that State may see fit to make. I want to know whether he stands to-day pledged to the abolition of slavery in the District of Columbia. I desire him to answer

---

[9] These resolutions, as it later was understood, were adopted at a local convention, preceding the first regular Republican convention by two years. See note on page 8.

whether he stands pledged to the prohibition of the slave trade between the different States. I desire to know whether he stands pledged to prohibit slavery in all the Territories of the United States, north as well as south of the Missouri Compromise line. I desire him to answer whether he is opposed to the acquisition of any more territory, unless slavery is prohibited therein. . . .

I ask Abraham Lincoln to answer these questions, in order that, when I trot him down to lower Egypt,[10] I may put the same questions to him. . . . In the remarks I have made on this platform, and the position of Mr. Lincoln upon it, I mean nothing personally disrespectful or unkind to that gentleman. I have known him for nearly twenty-five years. There were many points of sympathy between us when we first got acquainted. We were both comparatively boys, and both struggling with poverty in a strange land. I was a school-teacher in the town of Winchester, and he a flourishing grocery keeper in the town of Salem. He was more successful in his occupation than I was in mine, and hence more fortunate in this world's goods. Lincoln is one of those peculiar men who perform with admirable skill everything which they undertake. I made as good a school-teacher as I could, and when a cabinet-maker I made a good bedstead and tables, although my old boss said I succeeded better with bureaus and secretaries than with anything else; but I believe that Lincoln was always more successful in business than I, for his business enabled him to get into the Legislature. I met him there, however, and had a sympathy with him, because of the up-hill struggle we both had in life. He was then just as good at telling an anecdote as now. He could beat any of the boys wrestling, or running a foot-race, in pitching quoits or tossing a copper; could ruin more liquor than all of the boys of the town together; and the dignity and impartiality with which he presided at a horse-race or fist-fight excited the admiration and won the praise of everybody that was present and participated. I sympathized with him because he was struggling with difficulties, and so was I. . . .

---

[10] The lower part of Illinois was known as "Egypt," Some say it was so called because the people lived in darkness.

Having formed this new party for the benefit of deserters from Whiggery, and deserters from Democracy, and having laid down the Abolition platform which I have read, Lincoln now takes his stand and proclaims his Abolition doctrines. Let me read a part of them. In his speech at Springfield to the Convention which nominated him for the Senate, he said:—

"In my opinion it will not cease until a crisis shall have been reached and passed. 'A house divided against itself cannot stand.' I believe this government cannot endure permanently half slave and half free. I do not expect the Union to be dissolved,—I do not expect the house to fall; but I do expect it will cease to be divided. It will become all one thing, or all the other. Either the opponents of slavery will arrest the further spread of it, and place it where the public mind shall rest in the belief that it is in the course of ultimate extinction, or its advocates will push it forward till it shall become alike lawful in all the States,—old as well as new, North as well as South."

["Good," "Good," and cheers.]

I am delighted to hear you Black Republicans say "good." I have no doubt that doctrine expresses your sentiments, and I will prove to you now, if you will listen to me, that it is revolutionary and destructive of the existence of this Government. . . . I assert that uniformity in the local laws and institutions of the different States is neither possible nor desirable. If uniformity had been adopted when the Government was established, it must inevitably have been the uniformity of slavery everywhere, or else the uniformity of negro citizenship and negro equality everywhere.

We are told by Lincoln that he is utterly opposed to the Dred Scott decision, or will not submit to it, for the reason that he says it deprives the negro of the rights and privileges of citizenship. That is the first and main reason which he assigns for his warfare on the Supreme Court of the United States and its decision. I ask you, are you in favor of conferring upon the negro the rights and privileges of citizenship? Do you desire to strike out of our State Constitution that clause which keeps slaves and free negroes out of the State, and allow the free negroes to flow in, and cover your prairies with black settlements? Do you desire to turn this beautiful State into a free negro colony, in order that when Missouri abolishes slavery she can send one hundred thousand emancipated slaves into Illinois, to become citizens and voters, on an equality with yourselves? If you desire negro citizenship, if you desire to allow them to come into the State and settle with the white man, if you desire them to vote on an equality with yourselves, and to make them eligible to office, to serve on juries, and to adjudge your rights, then support Mr. Lincoln and the Black Republican party, who are in favor of the citizenship of the negro. For one, I am opposed to negro citizenship in any and every form. I believe this Government was made on the white basis. I believe it was made by white men, for the benefit of white men and their posterity forever, and I am in favor of confining citizenship to white men, men of European birth and descent, instead of conferring it upon negroes, Indians, and other inferior races. . . .

The question then arises, What rights and privileges are consistent with the public good? This is a question which each State and each Territory must decide for itself; Illinois has decided it for herself. We have provided that the negro shall not be a slave, and we have also provided that he shall not be a citizen, but protect him in his civil rights, in his life, his person, and his property, only depriving him of all political rights whatsoever, and refusing to put him on an equality with the white man. . . . But the Republicans say that he ought to be made a citizen, and when he becomes a citizen he becomes your equal, with all your rights and privileges. They assert the Dred Scott decision to be monstrous, because it denies that the negro is or can be a citizen under the Constitution. . . . Our fathers intended that our Constitutions should differ. They knew that the North and the South, having different climates, productions, and interests, required different institutions. This doctrine of Mr. Lincoln, of uniformity among the institutions of the different States, is a new doctrine, never dreamed of by Washington, Madison, or the framers of this Government. Mr. Lincoln and the Republican party set themselves up as wiser than these men who made this Government, which has flourished for seventy years under the principle of popular sovereignty, recognizing the right of each

State to do as it pleased. . . . I believe that this new doctrine preached by Mr. Lincoln and his party will dissolve the Union if it succeeds. They are trying to array all the Northern States in one body against the South, to excite a sectional war between the Free States and the Slave States, in order that the one or the other may be driven to the wall.

MR. LINCOLN'S REPLY

My Fellow Citizens: When a man hears himself somewhat misrepresented, it provokes him,—at least, I find it so with myself; but when misrepresentation becomes very gross and palpable, it is more apt to amuse him. The first thing I see fit to notice is the fact that Judge Douglas alleges, after running through the history of the old Democratic and the old Whig parties, that Judge Trumbull and myself made an arrangement in 1854, by which I was to have the place of General Shields[11] in the United States Senate, and Judge Trumbull was to have the place of Judge Douglas. Now, all I have to say upon that subject is, that I think no man—not even Judge Douglas— can prove it, because it is not true. I have no doubt he is "conscientious" in saying it. As to those resolutions that he took such a length of time to read, as being the platform of the Republican party in 1854, I say I never had anything to do with them, and I think Trumbull never had. Judge Douglas cannot show that either of us ever did have anything to do with them. . . .[12]

Now, gentlemen, I hate to waste my time on such things; but in regard to that general Abolition tilt that Judge Douglas makes, when he says that I was engaged at that time in selling out and Abolitionizing the old Whig party, I hope you will

---

[11] Gen. James Shields was U. S. Senator from Illinois, 1848–1854.

[12] Lincoln next explained that he was not in the Convention in 1854 which adopted these resolutions, although his name was signed as one of the committee, without consent. At the time he was attending court in Tazewell County and was not even in Springfield where the Convention was held.

permit me to read a part of a printed speech that I made then at Peoria, which will show altogether a different view of the position I took in that contest of 1854.

["Put on your specs."]

Yes, sir, I am obliged to do so; I am no longer a young man. . . .

When Southern people tell us they are no more responsible for the origin of slavery than we, I acknowledge the fact. When it is said that the institution exists, and that it is very difficult to get rid of it, in any satisfactory way, I can understand and appreciate the saying. I surely will not blame them for not doing what I should not know how to do myself. If all earthly power were given me, I should not know what to do, as to the existing institution. My first impulse would be to free all the slaves, and send them to Liberia—to their own native land. But a moment's reflection would convince me that whatever of high hope (as I think there is) there may be in this, in the long run, its sudden execution is impossible. If they were all landed there in a day they would all perish in the next ten days; and there are not surplus shipping and surplus money enough in the world to carry them there in many times ten days. What then? Free them all, and keep them among us as underlings? Is it quite certain that this betters their condition? I think I would not hold one in slavery, at any rate; yet the point is not clear enough to me to denounce people upon. What next? Free them, and make them politically and socially our equals? My own feelings will not admit of this; and if mine would, we well know that those of the great mass of white people will not. Whether this feeling accords with justice and sound judgment, is not the sole question, if indeed, it is any part of it. A universal feeling, whether well or ill-founded, cannot be safely disregarded. We cannot, then, make them equals. It does seem to me that systems of gradual emancipation might be adopted; but for their tardiness in this, I will not undertake to judge our brethren of the South. . . . .

But all this, to my judgment, furnishes no more excuse for permitting slavery to go into our own free territory than it would for reviving the African slave trade by law. The law which forbids the bringing of slaves from Africa, and that which has so long forbid the taking of them to Nebraska, can hardly be distinguished on any moral principle; and the repeal of the former could find quite as plausible excuses as that of the latter.

I have reason to know that Judge Douglas knows that I said this. I think he has the answer here to one of the questions he put to me. I do not mean to allow him to catechise me unless he pays back for it in kind. I will not answer questions one after another, unless he reciprocates; but as he has made this inquiry, and I have answered it before, he has got it without my getting anything in return. He has got my answer on the Fugitive Slave law.

Now, gentlemen, I don't want to read at any greater length; but this is the true complexion of all I have ever said in regard to the institution of slavery and the black race. This is the whole of it; and anything that argues me into his idea of perfect social and political equality with the negro is but a specious and fantastic arrangement of words, by which a man can prove a horse-chestnut to be a chestnut horse. I will say here, while upon this subject, that I have no purpose, directly or indirectly, to interfere with the institution of slavery in the States where it exists. I believe I have no lawful right to do so, and I have no inclination to do so. I have no purpose to introduce political and social equality between the white and the black races. There is a physical difference between the two which, in my judgment, will probably forever forbid their living together upon the footing of perfect equality; and inasmuch as it becomes a necessity there must be a difference, I, as well as Judge Douglas, am in favor of the race to which I belong having the superior position. I have never said anything to the contrary, but I hold that, notwithstanding all this, there is no reason in the world why the negro is not entitled to all the natural rights enumerated in the Declaration of Independence,—the right to life, liberty, and the pursuit of happiness. I hold that he is as much entitled to these as the white man. I agree with Judge Douglas he is not my equal in many respects,—certainly not in color, perhaps not in moral or intellectual endowment. But in the right to eat the bread, without the leave of anybody else, which his own hand earns, he is my equal, and the equal of Judge Douglas, and the equal of every living man. . . .

What is Popular Sovereignty?[13] Is it the right of the people to have slavery or not have it, as they see fit, in the Territories? I will state—and I have an able man to watch me—my understanding is that Popular Sovereignty, as now applied to the question of slavery, does allow the people of a Territory to have slavery if they want to, but does not allow them not to have it if they do not want it. I do not mean that if this vast concourse of people were in a Territory of the United States, any one of them would be obliged to have a slave if he did not want one; but I do say that, as I understand the Dred Scott decision, if any one man wants slaves, all the rest have no way of keeping that one man from holding them. . . .

Can it be true that placing this institution upon the original basis—the basis upon which our fathers placed it—can have any tendency to set the Northern and the Southern States at war with one another, or that it can have any tendency to make the people of Vermont raise sugar-cane, because they raise it in Louisiana, or that it can compel the people of Illinois to cut pine logs on the Grand Prairie,[14] where they will not grow, because they cut pine logs in Maine, where they do grow?. . . .

Henry Clay,[15] my beau ideal of a statesman, the man for whom I fought all my humble life,—Henry Clay once said of a class of men who would repress all tendencies to liberty and ultimate emancipation, that they must, if they would do this, go back to the era of our Independence, and muzzle the

---

[13] The theory that the citizens of a territory should decide at the time of forming a state constitution whether they would be free or slave was known as "popular sovereignty," or "squatter sovereignty"; that is, home rule for the settlers.

[14] A large prairie tract in central Illinois was known as the "Grand Prairie."

[15] Henry Clay of Kentucky (1777–1852) advocated a protective tariff, a free interpretation of the Constitution, and development of means of internal transportation. These were Whig principles, and he was the idol of the party.

cannon which thunders its annual joyous return; they must blow out the moral lights around us; they must penetrate the human soul, and eradicate there the love of liberty; and then, and not till then, could they perpetuate slavery in this country! To my thinking, Judge Douglas is, by his example and vast influence, doing that very thing in this community, when he says that the negro has nothing in the Declaration of Independence. Henry Clay plainly understood the contrary. Judge Douglas is going back to the era of our Revolution, and, to the extent of his ability, muzzling the cannon which thunders its annual joyous return. When he invites any people, willing to have slavery, to establish it, he is blowing out the moral lights around us. When he says he "cares not whether slavery is voted down or voted up,"—that it is a sacred right of self-government—he is, in my judgment, penetrating the human soul and eradicating the light of reason and the love of liberty in this American people. And now I will only say that when, by all these means and appliances, Judge Douglas shall succeed in bringing public sentiment to an exact accordance with his own views; when these vast assemblages shall echo back all these sentiments; when they shall come to repeat his views, and to avow his principles, and to say all that he says on these mighty questions,—then it needs only the formality of the second Dred Scott decision, which he indorses in advance, to make slavery alike lawful in all the States—old as well as new, North as well as South.

My friends, that ends the chapter. The judge can take his half-hour.

MR. DOUGLAS'S REPLY

Fellow Citizens: I will now occupy the half-hour allotted to me in replying to Mr. Lincoln. . . .

This denial[16] of his that he did not act on the committee, is a miserable quibble to avoid the main issue, which is, that

---

[16] Referring to the denial made by Lincoln that he was in the Springfield "Abolition" convention of 1854.

this Republican platform declares in favor of the unconditional repeal of the Fugitive Slave law. Has Lincoln answered whether he indorsed that or not? I called his attention to it when I first addressed you, and asked him for an answer, and I then predicted that he would not answer. How does he answer? Why, that he was not on the committee that wrote the resolutions. I then repeated the next proposition contained in the resolutions, which was to restrict slavery in those States in which it exists, and asked him whether he indorsed it. Does he answer yes, or no? He says in reply, "I was not on the committee at the time; I was up in Tazewell."

The next question I put to him was, whether he was in favor of prohibiting the admission of any more Slave States into the Union. I put the question to him distinctly, whether, if the people of the Territory, when they had sufficient population to make a State, should form their Constitution recognizing slavery, he would vote for or against its admission. He is a candidate for the United States Senate, and it is possible, if he should be elected, that he would have to vote directly on that question. I asked him to answer me and you, whether he would vote to admit a State into the Union, with slavery or without it, as its own people might choose. He did not answer that question. He dodges that question also, under the cover that he was not on the Committee at the time; that he was not present when the platform was made. I want to know if he should happen to be in the Senate when a State applied for admission, with a Constitution acceptable to her own people, would he vote to admit that State, if slavery was one of its institutions. He avoids the answer.

It is true he gives the Abolitionists to understand by a hint that he would not vote to admit such a State. And why? He goes on to say that the man who would talk about giving each State the right to have slavery or not, as it pleased, was akin to the man who would muzzle the guns which thundered forth the annual joyous return of the day of our Independence. He says that that kind of talk is casting a blight on the glory of this country. What is the meaning of that? That he is not in favor of each State to have the right of doing as it pleases on the slavery question? I will put the question to him again and again, and I intend to force it out of him. . . .

Now you see that upon these very points I am as far from bringing Mr. Lincoln up to the line as I ever was before. He does not want to avow his principles. I do want to avow mine, as clear as sunlight in midday. Democracy is founded upon the eternal principles of right. The plainer these principles are avowed before the people, the stronger will be the support which they will receive. I only wish I had the power to make them so clear that they would shine in the heavens for every man, woman, and child to read. The first of these principles that I would proclaim would be in opposition to Mr. Lincoln's doctrine of uniformity between the different States, and I would declare instead the sovereign right of each State to decide the slavery question as well as all other domestic questions for themselves, without interference from any other State or power whatsoever.

When that principle is recognized, you will have peace and harmony and fraternal feeling between all the States of this Union; until you do recognize that doctrine, there will be sectional warfare agitating and distracting the country. What does Mr. Lincoln propose? He says that the Union cannot exist divided into Free and Slave States. If it cannot endure thus divided, then he must strive to make them all Free or all Slave, which will inevitably bring about a dissolution of the Union.

Gentlemen, I am told that my time is out, and I am obliged to stop.

SECOND JOINT DEBATE

Freeport, August 27, 1858

MR. LINCOLN'S SPEECH

Ladies and Gentlemen: On Saturday last, Judge Douglas and myself first met in public discussion. He spoke one hour, I an hour and a half, and he replied for half an hour. The order is now reversed. I am to speak an hour, he an hour and a half, and then I am to reply for half an hour. I propose to devote myself during the first hour to the scope of what was brought within the range of his half-hour speech at Ottawa. . . .

I will take up the Judge's interrogatories as I find them printed in the Chicago *Times,* and answer them *seriatim.* In order that there may be no mistake about it, I have copied the interrogatories in writing, and also my answers to them. . . .

As to the first one, in regard to the Fugitive Slave law, I have never hesitated to say, and I do not now hesitate to say, that I think, under the Constitution of the United States, the people of the Southern States are entitled to a Congressional Fugitive Slave Law. Having said that, I have had nothing to say in regard to the existing Fugitive Slave Law, further than that I think it should have been framed so as to be free from some of the objections that pertain to it, without lessening its efficiency. And inasmuch as we are not now in an agitation in regard to an alteration or modification of that law, I would not be the man to introduce it as a new subject of agitation upon the general question of slavery.

In regard to the other question, of whether I am pledged to the admission of any more Slave States into the Union, I state to you very frankly that I would be exceedingly sorry ever to be put in a position of having to pass upon that question. I should be exceedingly glad to know that there would never be another Slave State admitted into the Union; but I must add, that if slavery shall be kept out of the Territories during the territorial existence of any one given Territory, and then the people shall, having a fair chance and a clear field, when they come to adopt the constitution, do such an extraordinary thing as to adopt a slave constitution, uninfluenced by the actual presence of the institution among them, I see no alternative, if we own the country, but to admit them into the Union.

The third interrogatory is answered by the answer to the second, it being, as I conceive, the same as the second.

The fourth one is in regard to the abolition of slavery in the District of Columbia. In relation to that, I have my mind very distinctly made up. I should be exceedingly glad to see slavery abolished in the District of Columbia. I believe that Congress possesses the constitutional power to abolish it. Yet as a member of Congress, I should not, with my present views, be in favor of endeavoring to abolish slavery in the District of Columbia, unless it would be upon these conditions: first, that the abolition should be gradual; second, that it should be on a vote of the majority of qualified voters in the District; and third, that compensation should be made to unwilling owners. With these three conditions, I confess I would be exceedingly glad to see Congress abolish slavery in the District of Columbia, and, in the language of Henry Clay, "sweep from our Capitol that foul blot upon our nation."

In regard to the fifth interrogatory, I must say here, that as to the question of the abolition of the slave trade between the different States, I can truly answer, as I have, that I am pledged to nothing about it. It is a subject to which I have not given that mature consideration that would make me feel authorized to state a position so as to hold myself entirely bound by it. In other words, that question has never been prominently enough before me to induce me to investigate whether we really have the constitutional power to do it. I could investigate it if I had sufficient time to bring myself to a conclusion upon that subject; but I have not done so, and I say so frankly to you here, and to Judge Douglas. I must say, however, that if I should be of opinion that Congress does possess the constitutional power to abolish the slave trade among the different States, I should still not be in favor of the exercise of that power unless upon some conservative principle, as I conceive it, akin to what I have said in relation to the abolition of slavery in the District of Columbia.

My answer as to whether I desire that slavery should be prohibited in all the Territories of the United States, is full and explicit within itself, and cannot be made clearer by any comments of mine. So I suppose in regard to the question whether I am opposed to the acquisition of any more territory unless slavery is first prohibited therein, my answer is such that I could add nothing by way of illustration, or making myself better understood, than the answer which I have placed in writing. . . .

I now proceed to propound to the Judge the interrogatories, so far as I have framed them. I will bring forward a new installment when I get them ready. I will bring them forward now only reaching to number four.

The first one is:—

Question 1.—If the people of Kansas shall, by means entirely unobjectionable in all other respects, adopt a State Constitution, and ask admission into the Union under it, before they have the requisite number of inhabitants according to the English bill,—some ninety-three thousand,—will you vote to admit them?

Question 2. Can the people of a United States Territory, in any lawful way, against the wish of any citizen of the United States, exclude slavery from its limits prior to the formation of a State Constitution?[17]

Question 3. If the Supreme Court of the United States shall decide that States cannot exclude slavery from their limits, are

---

[17] This is thought to be the most important of all questions put to Douglas by Lincoln.

you in favor of acquiescing in, adopting, and following such decision as a rule of political action?

Question 4. Are you in favor of acquiring additional territory, in disregard of how such acquisition may affect the nation on the slavery question? . . . .

Go on, Judge Douglas.

MR. DOUGLAS'S SPEECH

Ladies and Gentlemen: The silence with which you have listened to Mr. Lincoln during his hour is creditable to this vast audience, composed of men of various political parties. Nothing is more honorable to any large mass of people assembled for the purpose of a fair discussion, than that kind and respectful attention that is yielded not only to your political friends, but to those who are opposed to you in politics.

I am glad that at last I have brought Mr. Lincoln to the conclusion that he had better define his position on certain political questions to which I called his attention at Ottawa. He there showed no disposition, no inclination, to answer them. I did not present idle questions for him to answer merely for my gratification. I laid the foundation for those interrogatories by showing that they constituted the platform of the party whose nominee he is for the Senate. I did not presume that I had the right to catechise him as I saw proper, unless I showed that his party, or a majority of it, stood upon the platform and were in favor of the propositions upon which my questions were based. I desired simply to know, inasmuch as he had been nominated as the first, last, and only choice of his party, whether he concurred in the platform which that party had adopted for its government. In a few moments I will proceed to review the answers which he has given to these interrogatories; but, in order to relieve his anxiety, I will first respond to these which he has presented to me. Mark you, he has not presented interrogatories which have ever received the sanction of the party with which I am acting, and hence he has no other foundation for them than his own curiosity.

First, he desires to know, if the people of Kansas shall form a constitution by means entirely proper and unobjectionable, and ask admission into the Union as a State, before they have the requisite population for a member of Congress, whether I will vote for that admission. I will answer his question. In reference to Kansas, it is my opinion that as she has population enough to constitute a Slave State, she has people enough for a Free State. I will not make Kansas an exceptional case to the other States of the Union. I hold it to be a sound rule, of universal application, to require a Territory to contain the requisite population. . . . On another occasion I proposed that neither Kansas nor any other Territory should be admitted until it had the requisite population. Congress did not adopt any of my propositions containing this general rule, but did make an exception of Kansas. I will stand by that exception. Either Kansas must come in as a Free State, with whatever population she may have, or the rule must be applied to all the other Territories alike. I therefore answer at once, that, it having been decided that Kansas has people enough for a Slave State, I hold that she has enough for a Free State. I hope Mr. Lincoln is satisfied with my answer; and now I would like to get his answer to his own interrogatory,—whether or not he will vote to admit Kansas before she has the requisite population. I want to know whether he will vote to admit Oregon before that Territory has the requisite population. I would like Mr. Lincoln to answer this question. I would like him to take his own medicine.

The next question propounded to me by Mr. Lincoln is, Can the people of a Territory, in any lawful way, against the wishes of any citizen of the United States, exclude slavery from their limits prior to the formation of a State Constitution? I answer emphatically, as Mr. Lincoln has heard me answer a hundred times from every stump in Illinois, that in my opinion the people of a Territory can, by lawful means, exclude slavery from their limits prior to the formation of a State Constitution[18]. . . . It matters not what way the Supreme Court

---

[18] This is the affirmative reply of Douglas to the important question of Lincoln.

may hereafter decide as to the abstract question whether slavery may or may not go into a Territory under the Constitution, the people have the lawful means to introduce it or exclude it as they please, for the reason that slavery cannot exist a day or an hour anywhere, unless it is supported by local police regulations. Those police regulations can only be established by the local legislature; and if the people are opposed to slavery, they will elect representatives to that body who will by unfriendly legislation effectually prevent the introduction of it into their midst. If, on the contrary, they are for it, their legislature will favor its extension. Hence, no matter what the decision of the Supreme Court may be on that abstract question, still the right of the people to make a Slave Territory or a Free Territory is perfect and complete under the Nebraska bill. I hope Mr. Lincoln deems my answer satisfactory on that point.

The third question which Mr. Lincoln presented is, If the Supreme Court of the United States shall decide that a State of this Union cannot exclude slavery from its own limits, will I submit to it? I am amazed that Lincoln should ask such a question.

["A school-boy knows better."]

Yes, a school-boy does know better. Mr. Lincoln's object is to cast an imputation upon the Supreme Court. He might as well ask me, Suppose Mr. Lincoln should steal a horse, would I sanction it; and it would be as genteel in me to ask him, in the event he stole a horse, what ought to be done with him. He casts an imputation upon the Supreme Court of the United States, by supposing that they would violate the Constitution of the United States. I tell him that such a thing is not possible. It would be an act of moral treason that no man on the bench could ever descend to. Mr. Lincoln himself would never in his partial feelings so far forget what was right as to be guilty of such an act.

The fourth question of Mr. Lincoln is, Are you in favor of acquiring additional territory, in disregard as to how such acquisition may affect the Union on the slavery question? This question is very ingeniously and cunningly put.

The Black Republican creed lays it down expressly, that under no circumstances shall we acquire any more territory, unless slavery is first prohibited in the country. I ask Mr. Lincoln whether he is in favor of that proposition. Are you (addressing Mr. Lincoln) opposed to the acquisition of any more territory, under any circumstances, unless slavery is prohibited in it? That he does not like to answer. When I ask him whether he stands up to that article in the platform of his party, he turns, Yankee-fashion, and without answering it, asks me whether I am in favor of acquiring territory without regard to how it may affect the Union on the slavery question. I answer, that whenever it becomes necessary, in our growth and progress, to acquire more territory, that I am in favor of it, without reference to the question of slavery; and when we have acquired it, I will leave the people free to do as they please, either to make it slave or free territory, as they prefer. . . .

I trust now that Mr. Lincoln will deem himself answered on his four points. He racked his brain so much in devising these four questions that he exhausted himself, and had not strength enough to invent the others. As soon as he is able to hold a council with his advisers, Lovejoy, Farnsworth, and Fred Douglass,[19] he will frame and propound others.

["Good, Good."]

You Black Republicans who say "good," I have no doubt think that they are all good men. I have reason to recollect that some people in this country think that Fred Douglass is a very good man. The last time I came here to make a speech, while talking from the stand to you people of Freeport, as I am doing to-day, I saw a carriage—and a magnificent one it was—drive up and take a position on the outside of the crowd; a beautiful young lady was sitting on the box-seat, while Fred Douglass

---

[19] Lovejoy and Farnsworth were Abolitionist leaders of Illinois. Fred Douglass was a free negro of unusual ability. In citing these men as Lincoln's advisers, Douglas is emphasizing Lincoln's supposed connection with the obnoxious Abolitionists.

and her mother reclined inside and the owner of the carriage acted as driver. I saw this in your own town.

["What of it?"]

All I have to say of it is this, that if you Black Republicans think that the negro ought to be on a social equality with your wives and daughters, and ride in a carriage with your wife, whilst you drive the team, you have perfect right to do so. I am told that one of Fred Douglass' kinsmen, another rich black negro, is now traveling in this part of the State making speeches for his friend Lincoln as the champion of the black men.

["What have you to say against it?"]

All I have to say on that subject is, that those of you who believe that the negro is your equal and ought to be on an equality with you socially, politically, and legally, have a right to entertain those opinions, and of course will vote for Mr. Lincoln. . . .

Now, there are a great many Black Republicans of you who do not know this thing was done.

["White, white," and great clamor.]

I wish to remind you that while Mr. Lincoln was speaking there was not a Democrat vulgar and blackguard enough to interrupt him. But I know that the shoe is pinching you. I am clinching Lincoln now, and you are scared to death for the result. I have seen this thing before. I have seen men make appointments for joint discussions, and the moment their man has been heard, try to interrupt and prevent a fair hearing of the other side. I have seen your mobs before, and defy your wrath. [Tremendous applause.]

My friends, do not cheer, for I need my whole time. . . .

Mr. Lincoln lays down the doctrine that this Union cannot endure divided as our fathers made it, with Free and Slave States. He says they must all become one thing, or all the other; that they must all be free or all slave, or else the Union cannot continue to exist; it being his opinion that to admit any more Slave States, to continue to divide the Union into Free and Slave States, will dissolve it. I want to know of Mr. Lincoln whether he will vote for the admission of another Slave State.

He tells you the Union cannot exist unless the States are all
free or all slave; he tells you that he is opposed to making them
all slave, and hence he is for making them all free, in order that
the Union may exist; and yet he will not say that he will not
vote against another Slave State, knowing that the Union must
be dissolved if he votes for it. I ask you if that is fair dealing. . . . . Show me that it is my duty, in order to save the
Union, to do a particular act, and I will do it if the Constitution
does not prohibit it. I am not for the dissolution of the Union
under any circumstances. I will pursue no course of conduct
that will give just cause for the dissolution of the Union. The
hope of the friends of freedom throughout the world rests
upon the perpetuity of this Union. The down-trodden and
oppressed people who are suffering under European despotism
all look with hope and anxiety to the American Union as the
only resting place and permanent home of freedom and
self-government. . . .

I know Mr. Lincoln's object; he wants to divide the
Democratic party, in order that he may defeat me and get to
the Senate. . . .

MR. LINCOLN'S REJOINDER

My Friends: It will readily occur to you that I cannot, in half
an hour, notice all the things that so able a man as Judge
Douglas can say in an hour and a half; and I hope, therefore,
if there be anything that he has said upon which you would
like to hear something from me, but which I omit to com-
ment upon, you will bear in mind that it would be expecting
an impossibility for me to go over his whole ground. I can
but take up some of the points that he has dwelt upon, and
employ my half-hour specially on them.

The first thing I have to say to you is a word in regard to
Judge Douglas's declaration about the "vulgarity and blackguardism" in the audience,—that no such thing, as he says,
was shown by any Democrat while I was speaking. Now, I
only wish, by way of reply on this subject, to say that while I

was speaking, I used no "vulgarity or blackguardism" toward any Democrat. . . .

He says I do not declare I would in any event vote for the admission of a Slave State into the Union. If I have been fairly reported, he will see that I did give an explicit answer to his interrogatories; I did not merely say that I would dislike to be put to the test, but I said clearly, if I were put to the test, and a Territory from which slavery had been excluded should present herself with a State Constitution sanctioning slavery,— a most extraordinary thing and wholly unlikely to happen,—I did not see how I could avoid voting for her admission. But he refuses to understand that I said so, and he wants this audience to understand that I did not say so. Yet it will be so reported in the printed speech that he cannot help seeing it.

He says if I should vote for the admission of a Slave State I would be voting for a dissolution of the Union, because I hold that the Union cannot permanently exist half slave and half free. I repeat that I do not believe this Government can endure permanently half slave and half free; yet I do not admit, nor does it at all follow, that the admission of a single Slave State will permanently fix the character and establish this as a universal slave nation. The Judge is very happy indeed at working up these quibbles. . . .

His hope rested on the idea of enlisting the great "Black Republican" party, and making it the tail of his new kite. He knows he was expecting from day to day to turn Republican and place himself at the head of our organization. He has found that these despised "Black Republicans" estimate him by a standard which he has taught them none too well. Hence he is crawling back into his old camp, and you will find him eventually installed in full fellowship among those whom he was then battling, and with whom he now pretends to be at such fearful variance.

[Loud applause and cries of "Go on, Go on."]

I cannot, gentlemen, my time has expired.

THIRD JOINT DEBATE

Jonesboro, September 15, 1858

MR. DOUGLAS'S SPEECH

Ladies and Gentlemen: I appear before you to-day in pursuance of a previous notice, and have made arrangements with Mr. Lincoln to divide time, and discuss with him the leading political topics that now agitate the country.

Prior to 1854 this country was divided into two great political parties known as Whig and Democratic. Since that period, a great revolution has taken place in the formation of parties, by which they now seem to be divided by a geographical line, a large party in the North being arrayed under the Abolition or Republican banner, in hostility to the Southern States, Southern people, and Southern institutions. . . .

They were Republicans or Abolitionists in the North, anti-Nebraska men down about Springfield, and in this neighborhood they contented themselves with talking about the inexpediency of the repeal of the Missouri Compromise. In the extreme northern counties they brought out men to canvass the State whose complexion suited their political creed; and hence Fred Douglass, the negro, was to be found there, following General Cass,[20] and attempting to speak on behalf of

---

[20] Senator Lewis Cass of Michigan, a Democratic candidate for the presidency in 1848, was defeated by Gen. Zachary Taylor, a Whig.

Lincoln, Trumbull, and Abolitionism, against that illustrious Senator. Why, they brought Fred Douglass to Freeport, when I was addressing a meeting there, in a carriage driven by the white owner, the negro sitting inside with the white lady and her daughter. . . .

Mr. Lincoln likens that bond of the Federal Constitution, joining Free and Slave States together, to a house divided against itself, and says that it is contrary to the law of God, and cannot stand. When did he learn, and by what authority does he proclaim, that this Government is contrary to the law of God and cannot stand? It has stood thus divided into Free and Slave States from its organization up to this day. During that period we have increased from four millions to thirty millions of people; we have extended our territory from the Mississippi to the Pacific Ocean; we have acquired the Floridas and Texas, and other territory sufficient to double our geographical extent; we have increased in population, in wealth, and in power beyond any example on earth; we have risen from a weak and feeble power to become the terror and admiration of the civilized world; and all this has been done under a Constitution which Mr. Lincoln, in substance, says is in violation of the law of God; and under a Union divided into Free and Slave States, which Mr. Lincoln thinks, because of such division, cannot stand. Surely, Mr. Lincoln is a wiser man than those who framed the Government. . . .

I hold that a negro is not and never ought to be a citizen of the United States. I hold that this Government was made on the white basis, by white men, for the benefit of white men and their posterity forever, and should be administered by white men and none others. I do not believe that the Almighty made the negro capable of self-government. I am aware that all the Abolition lecturers that you find traveling about through the country are in the habit of reading the Declaration of Independence to prove that all men were created equal and endowed by their Creator with certain inalienable rights, among which are life, liberty, and the pursuit of happiness. Mr. Lincoln is very much in the habit of following in the track of Lovejoy in this particular, by reading that part of the Declaration of Independence to prove that the negro was endowed by the Almighty with inalienable right of equality with white men. Now, I say to you, my fellow-citizens, that in my opinion, the signers of the Declaration had no reference to the negro whatever, when they declared all men to be created equal. They desired to express by that phrase white men, men of European birth and European descent, and had no reference either to the negro, the savage Indians, the Fiji, the Malay, or any other inferior and degraded race, when they spoke of the equality of men. One great evidence that such was their understanding, is to be found in the fact that at that time every one of the thirteen colonies was a slave-holding colony, every signer of the Declaration represented a slaveholding constituency, and we know that not one of them emancipated his slaves, much less offered citizenship to them, when they signed the Declaration; and yet, if they intended to declare that the negro was the equal of the white man, and entitled by divine right to an equality with him, they were bound, as honest men, that day and hour to have put their negroes on an equality with themselves. Instead of doing so, with uplifted eyes to Heaven they implored the divine blessing upon them, during the seven years' bloody war they had to fight to maintain that Declaration, never dreaming that they were violating divine law by still holding the negroes in bondage and depriving them of equality.

My friends, I am in favor of preserving this Government as our fathers made it. It does not follow by any means that because a negro is not your equal or mine, that hence he must necessarily be a slave. On the contrary, it does follow that we ought to extend to the negro every right, every privilege, every immunity, which he is capable of enjoying, consistent with the good of society. When you ask me what these rights are, what their nature and extent is, I tell you that is a question which each State of this Union must decide for itself. . . .

I now come back to the question, why cannot this Union exist forever, divided into Free and Slave States, as our fathers made it? It can thus exist if each State will carry out the principles upon which our institutions were founded; to wit, the rights of each State to do as it pleases, without meddling with its neighbors. Just act upon that great principle, and this Union will not only live forever, but it will extend and expand until it covers the whole continent, and makes this confederacy one grand, ocean-bound Republic. We must bear in mind that we are yet a young nation, growing with a rapidity unequalled in the history of the world, that our national increase is great, and that the emigration from the old world is increasing, requiring us to expand and acquire new territory from time to time, in order to give our people land to live upon. If we live upon the principle of State rights and State sovereignity, each State regulating its own affairs and minding its own business, we can go on and extend indefinitely, just as fast and as far as we need the territory. . . .

MR. LINCOLN'S REPLY

Ladies and Gentlemen: There is very much in the principles that Judge Douglas has here enunciated that I must cordially approve, and over which I shall have no controversy with him. In so far as he has insisted that all the States have the right to do exactly as they please about all their domestic relations, including that of slavery, I agree entirely with him. He places me wrong in spite of all I can tell him, though I repeat it again and again, insisting that I have no difference with him upon this subject. I have made a great many speeches, some of which have been printed, and it will be utterly impossible for him to find anything that I have ever put in print contrary to what I now say upon this subject. I hold myself under constitutional obligations to allow the people in all the States, without interference, direct or indirect, to do exactly as they please; and I deny that I have any inclination to interfere with them, even if there were no such constitutional obligation. I can only say again that I am placed improperly—altogether improperly, in spite of all I can say—when it is insisted that I entertain any other view or purposes in regard to that matter.

While I am upon this subject, I will make some answers briefly to certain propositions that Judge Douglas has put. He says, "Why can't this Union endure permanently, half slave and half free?" I have said that I supposed it could not, and I will try, before this new audience, to give briefly some of the reasons for entertaining that opinion. Another form of his question is, "Why can't we let it stand as our fathers placed it?" That is the exact difficulty between us. I say that Judge Douglas and his friends have changed it from the position in which our fathers originally placed it. I say, in the way our fathers originally left the slavery question, the institution was in the course of ultimate extinction, and the public mind rested in the belief that it was in the course of ultimate extinction. I say, when this Government was first established, it was the policy of its founders to prohibit the spread of slavery into the new Territories of the United States, where it had not existed. But Judge Douglas and his friends have broken up that policy, and placed it upon a new basis, by which it is to become national and perpetual. All I have asked or desired anywhere is that it should be placed back again upon the basis that the fathers of our Government originally placed it upon. I have no doubt that it would become extinct, for all time to come, if we but re-adopted the policy of the fathers, by restricting it to the limits it has already covered,—restricting it from the new Territories. . . .

He also says that the Whig party in National Convention agreed to abide by and regard as a finality the Compromise of 1850. . . .

When that Compromise was made it did not repeal the old Missouri Compromise. It left a region of United States territory half as large as the present territory of the United States, north of the line of 36 degrees 30 minutes, in which slavery was prohibited by act of Congress. This Compromise did not repeal that one. It did not affect or propose to repeal it. But at last it became Judge Douglas's duty, as he thought (and I find no fault with him), as Chairman of the Committee on Territories, to bring in a bill for the organization of a Territorial

Government,—first of one, then of two Territories[21] north of
that line. When he did so it ended in his inserting a provision
substantially repealing the Missouri Compromise. That was
because the Compromise of 1850 had not repealed it. And
now I ask why he could not have let that Compromise alone?
We were quiet from the agitation of the slavery question. We
were making no fuss about it. All had acquiesced in the
Compromise measures of 1850. We never had been seriously
disturbed by an Abolition agitation before that period. When
he came to form governments for the Territories north of the
line of 36 degrees, 30 minutes, why could he not have let that
matter stand as it was standing? Was it necessary to the organization of a Territory? Not at all. Iowa lay north of the line, and
had been organized as a Territory, and come into the Union as
a State, without disturbing that Compromise. There was no
sort of necessity for destroying it to organize these Territories.
But, gentlemen, it would take up all my time to meet all the
little quibbling arguments of Judge Douglas to show that the
Missouri Compromise was repealed by the Compromise of
1850. My own opinion is, that a careful investigation of all the
arguments to sustain the position that that Compromise was
virtually repealed by the Compromise of 1850 would show
that they are the merest fallacies. . . .

In complaining of what I said in my speech at Springfield, in
which he says I accepted my nomination for the Senatorship
(where, by the way, he is at fault, for if he will examine it, he
will find no acceptance in it), he again quotes that portion in
which I said that "a house divided against itself cannot stand."
Let me say a word in regard to that matter. He tries to persuade
us that there must be a variety in the different institutions of the
States of the Union; that that variety necessarily proceeds from
the variety of soil, climate, of the face of the country, and the
difference in the natural features of the States. I agree to all that.
Have these very matters ever produced any difficulty amongst
us? Not at all. Have we ever had any quarrel over the fact that

---

[21] Kansas and Nebraska.

they have laws in Louisiana designed to regulate the commerce that springs from the production of sugar? Or because we have a different class relative to the production of flour in this State? Have they produced any differences? Not at all. They are the very cements of this Union. They don't make the house a "house divided against itself." They are the props that hold up the house and sustain the Union.

But has it been so with this element of slavery? Have we not always had quarrels and difficulties over it? And when will we cease to have quarrels over it? Like causes produce like effects. It is worth while to observe that we have generally had comparative peace upon the slavery question, and that there has been no cause for alarm until it was excited by the effort to spread it into new territory. Whenever it has been limited to its present bounds, and there has been no effort to spread it, there has been peace. All the trouble and convulsion has proceeded from efforts to spread it over more territory. It was thus at the date of the Missouri Compromise. It was so again with the annexation of Texas; so with the territory acquired by the Mexican War; and it is so now. Whenever there has been an effort to spread it there has been agitation and resistance. Now, I appeal to this audience (very few of whom are my political friends), as national men, whether we have reason to expect that the agitation in regard to this subject will cease while the causes that tend to reproduce agitation are actively at work? Will not the same cause that produced agitation in 1820, when the Missouri Compromise was formed,—that which produced the agitation upon the annexation of Texas, and at other times,—work out the same results always? Do you think that the nature of man will be changed, that the same causes that produced agitation at one time will not have the same effect at another?

This has been the result so far as my observation of the slavery question and my reading in history extends. What right have we, then, to hope that the trouble will cease, that the agitation will come to an end, until it shall either be placed back where it originally stood, and where the fathers originally placed it, or, on the other hand, until it shall entirely master all opposition? This is the view I entertain, and this is the reason why I entertained it, as Judge Douglas has read from my Springfield speech. . . .

At Freeport I answered several interrogatories that had been propounded to me by Judge Douglas at the Ottawa meeting. The Judge has not yet seen fit to find any fault with the position that I took in regard to those seven interrogatories, which were certainly broad enough, in all conscience, to cover the entire ground. In my answers, which have been printed, and all have had the opportunity of seeing, I take the ground that those who elect me must expect that I will do nothing which will not be in accordance with those answers. I have some right to assert that Judge Douglas has no fault to find with them. But he chooses to still try to thrust me upon different ground, without paying any attention to my answers, the obtaining of which from me cost him so much trouble and concern. At the same time I propounded four interrogatories to him, claiming it as a right that he should answer as many interrogatories for me as I did for him, and I would reserve myself for a future installment when I got them ready. The Judge, in answering me upon that occasion, put in what I suppose he intends as answers to all four of my interrogatories. . . .

The second interrogatory that I propounded to him was this:—

Question 2. Can the people of a United States Territory, in any lawful way, against the wish of any citizen of the United States, exclude slavery from its limits prior to the formation of a State Constitution?

To this Judge Douglas answered that they can lawfully exclude slavery from the Territory prior to the formation of a Constitution. He goes on to tell us how it can be done. As I understand him, he holds that it can be done by the Territorial Legislature refusing to make any enactments for the protection of slavery in the Territory, and especially by adopting unfriendly legislation to it. For the sake of clearness, I state it again: that they can exclude slavery from the Territory, 1st, by witholding what he assumes to be an indispensable assistance to it in the way of legislation; and, 2nd, by unfriendly legislation. If I rightly understood him, I wish to ask your attention for a while to his position.

In the first place, the Supreme Court of the United States has decided that any Congressional prohibition of slavery in the Territories is unconstitutional, that they have reached this proposition as a conclusion from their former proposition, that the Constitution of the United States expressly recognizes property in slaves, and from that other Constitutional provision, that no person shall be deprived of property without due process of law. Hence, they reach the conclusion that as the Constitution of the United States expressly recognizes property in slaves, and prohibits any person from being deprived of property without due process of law, to pass an Act of Congress by which a man who owned a slave on one side of a line would be deprived of him if he took him on the other side, is depriving him of that property without due process of law. That I understand to be the decision of the Supreme Court. I understand also that Judge Douglas adheres most firmly to that decision; and the difficulty is, how is it possible for any power to exclude slavery from the Territory, unless in violation of that decision? That is the difficulty. . . .

I hold that the proposition that slavery cannot enter a new country without police regulations is historically false. It is not true at all. I hold that the history of this country shows that the institution of slavery was originally planted upon this continent without these "police regulations" which the Judge now thinks necessary for the actual establishment of it. Not only so, but is there not another fact: how came this Dred Scott decision to be made? It was made upon the case of a negro being taken and actually held in slavery in Minnesota Territory, claiming his freedom because the act of Congress prohibited his being so held there. Will the Judge pretend that Dred Scott was not held there without police regulations? There is at least one matter of record as to his having been held in slavery in the Territory, not only without police regulations, but in the teeth of Congressional legislation supposed to be valid at the time. This shows that there is vigor enough in slavery to plant itself in a new country even against unfriendly legislation. It takes not only law, but the enforcement of law, to keep it out. . . .

My fifth interrogatory is this:

If the slaveholding citizens of a United States Territory should need and demand Congressional legislation for the protection of their slave property in such Territory, would you, as a member of Congress, vote for or against such legislation?

Judge Douglas: Will you repeat that? I want to answer that question.

Mr. Lincoln: If the slaveholding citizens of a United States Territory should need and demand Congressional legislation for the protection of their slave property in such Territory, would you, as a member of Congress, vote for or against such legislation?

I am aware that in some of the speeches Judge Douglas has made he has spoken as if he did not know or think that the Supreme Court had decided that a Territorial Legislature cannot exclude slavery. Precisely what the Judge would say upon the subject, whether he would say definitely that he does not understand they have so decided, or whether he would say he does understand that the court have so decided,—I do not know; but I know that in his speech at Springfield he spoke of it as a thing they had not decided yet; and in his answer to me at Freeport he spoke of it, so far, again, as I can comprehend it, as a thing that had not yet been decided. Now I hold that if the Judge does entertain that view, I think that he is not mistaken in so far as it can be said that the court has not decided anything save the mere question of jurisdiction. I know the legal arguments that can be made,—that after a court has decided that it cannot take jurisdiction in a case, it then has decided all that is before it, and that is the end of it. A plausible argument can be made in favor of that proposition; but I know that Judge Douglas has said in one of his speeches that the court went forward, like honest men as they were, and decided all the points in the case. If any points are really extra-judicially decided, because not necessarily before them, then this one as to the power of the Territorial Legislature to exclude slavery is one of them, as also the one that the Missouri Compromise was null and void. They are both extra-judicial, or neither is, according as the court held that they had no jurisdiction in the case between the parties, because of want of capacity of one party to maintain a suit in that court. I want, if I have sufficient time, to show that the court did pass its opinion; but that is the only thing actually done in the case. If they did not decide, they showed what they were ready to decide whenever the matter was before them. What is that opinion? After having argued that Congress had no power to pass a law excluding slavery from a United States Territory, they then used language to this effect: That inasmuch as Congress itself could not exercise such a power, it followed as a matter of course that it could not authorize a Territorial Government to exercise it; for the Territorial Legislature can do no more than Congress could do. Thus it expressed its opinion emphatically against the power of a Territorial Legislature to exclude slavery, leaving us in just as little doubt on that point as upon any other point they really decided.

Now, my fellow-citizens, I will detain you only a little while longer; my time is nearly out. I find a report of a speech made by Judge Douglas at Joliet, since we last met at Freeport—published, I believe, in the Missouri *Republican*—on the 9th of this month, in which Judge Douglas says:

You know at Ottawa, I read this platform, and asked him if he concurred in each and all of the principles set forth in it. He would not answer these questions. At last I said frankly, I wish you to answer them, because when I get them up here where the color of your principles are a little darker than in Egypt, I intend to trot you down to Jonesboro. The very notice that I was going to take him down to Egypt made him tremble in the knees so that he had to be carried from the platform. He laid up seven days, and in the meantime held a consultation with all his political physicians; they had Lovejoy, and Farnsworth, and all the leaders of the Abolition party; they consulted it all over, and at last Lincoln came to the conclusion that he would answer, so he came up to Freeport last Friday.

Now, that statement altogether furnishes a subject for philosophical contemplation. I have been treating it in that way, and I have really come to the conclusion that I can explain it in no other way than by believing the Judge is crazy. If he was in his right mind, I cannot conceive how he would have risked disgusting the four or five thousand of his own friends who stood there, and knew, as to my having been carried from the platform, that there was not a word of truth in it.

Judge Douglas: Didn't they carry you off?

Mr. Lincoln: There that question illustrates the character of this man Douglas exactly. He smiles now and says, "Didn't they carry you off?" But he said then, "he had to be carried off;" and he said it to convince the country that he had so completely broken me down by his speech that I had to be carried away.[22] Now he seeks to dodge it, and asks, "Didn't they carry you off?" Yes, they did. But, Judge Douglas, why didn't you tell the truth? I would like to know why you didn't tell the truth about it. And then again, "He laid up seven days." He put this in print for the people of the country to read as a serious document. . . . There is another thing in that statement that alarmed me very greatly as he states it, that he was going to "trot me down to Egypt." Thereby he would have you to infer that I would not come to Egypt unless he forced me,— that I could not be got here, unless he, giant-like, had hauled me down here. That statement he makes, too, in the teeth of the knowledge that I had made the stipulation to come down here, and that he himself had been very reluctant to enter into the stipulation. More than all this, Judge Douglas, when he made that statement, must have been crazy, and wholly out of his sober senses, or else he would have known that when he got me down here, that promise—that windy promise—of his

---

[22] In truth, Lincoln's enthusiastic friends carried him on their shoulders at the close of the Ottawa debate.

powers to annihilate me, wouldn't amount to anything. Now, how little do I look like being carried away trembling? Let the Judge go on; and after he is done with his half hour, I want you all, if I can't go home myself, to let me stay and rot here; and if anything happens to the Judge, if I cannot carry him to the hotel and put him to bed, let me stay here and rot. I say, then, there is something extraordinary in this statement. I ask you if you know any other living man who would make such a statement? I will ask my friend Casey, over there, if he would do such a thing? Would he send that out, and have his men take it as the truth? Did the Judge talk of trotting me down to Egypt to scare me to death? Why, I know this people better than he does. I was raised just a little east of here. I am a part of this people. But the Judge was raised further north, and perhaps he has some horrid idea of what this people might be induced to do. But really, I have talked about this matter perhaps longer than I ought, for it is no great thing; and yet the smallest are often the most difficult things to deal with. The Judge has set about seriously trying to make the impression that when we meet at different places I am literally in his clutches,—that I am a poor, helpless, decrepit mouse, and that I can do nothing at all. This is one of the ways he has taken to create that impression. I don't know any other way to meet it, except this. I don't want to quarrel with him,—to call him a liar; but when I come square up to him I don't know what else to call him, if I must tell the truth out. I want to be at peace and reserve all my fighting powers for necessary occasions. My time, now, is very nearly out, and I give up the trifle that is left to the Judge, to let him set my knees trembling again, if he can.

MR. DOUGLAS'S REPLY

My Friends: While I am very grateful to you for the enthusiasm which you show for me, I will say in all candor, that your quietness will be much more agreeable than your applause, inasmuch as you deprive me of some part of my time whenever you cheer.

I will commence where Mr. Lincoln left off, and make a remark upon this serious complaint of his about my speech at Joliet. I did say there in a playful manner that when I put these questions to Mr. Lincoln at Ottawa he failed to answer, and that he trembled and had to be carried off the stand, and required seven days to get up his reply. That he did not walk off from that stand, he will not deny. That when the crowd went away from the stand with me, a few persons carried him home on their shoulders and laid him down, he will admit. I wish to say to you that whenever I degrade my friends and myself by allowing them to carry me on their backs along through the public streets, when I am able to walk, I am willing to be deemed crazy. . . .

In the first place, Mr. Lincoln says he would be exceedingly sorry to be put in a position where he would have to vote on the question of the admission of a Slave State. Why is he a candidate for the Senate if he would be sorry to be put in that position? I trust the people of Illinois will not put him in a position which he would be so sorry to occupy. The next position he takes is that he would be glad to know that there would never be another Slave State, yet in certain contingencies, he might have to vote for one. What is that contingency? "If Congress keeps slavery out by law while it is a Territory, and then the people should have a fair chance and should adopt slavery, uninfluenced by the presence of the institution," he supposed he would have to admit the State. Suppose Congress should not keep slavery out during their territorial existence, then how would he vote when the people applied for admission into the Union with a slave constitution? That he does not answer; and that is the condition of every Territory we have now got. Slavery is not kept out of Kansas by act of Congress; and when I put the question to Mr. Lincoln, whether he will vote for the admission with or without slavery, as her people may desire, he will not answer, and you have not got an answer from him. In Nebraska, slavery is not prohibited by act of Congress, but the people are allowed, under the Nebraska bill, to do as they please on the subject; and when I ask him whether he will vote to admit Nebraska with a slave constitution if her people desire it, he will not answer. So with New Mexico, Washington Territory, Arizona, and the four new States to be admitted from Texas.[23] You cannot get an answer from him to these questions. His answer only applies to a given case, to a condition,—things which he knows do not exist in any one Territory in the Union. He tries to give you to understand that he would allow the people to do as they please, and yet he dodges the question as to every Territory in the Union. I now ask why cannot Mr. Lincoln answer as to each of these Territories? He has not done it, and he will not do it. The Abolitionists up North understand that this answer is made with a view of not committing himself on any one Territory now in existence. It is so understood there, and you cannot expect an answer from him on a case that applies to any one Territory, or applies to the new States which by compact we are pledged to admit out of Texas, when they have the requisite population and desire admission. I submit to you whether he has made a frank answer, so that you can tell how he would vote in any one of these cases. "He would be sorry to be put in the position." Why would he be sorry to be put in this position, if his duty required him to give the vote? If the people of a Territory ought to be permitted to come into the Union as a State, with slavery or without it, as they pleased, why not give the vote admitting them, cheerfully? If in his opinion they ought not to come in with slavery, even if they wanted to, why not say that he would cheerfully vote against their admission? His intimation is that conscience would not let him vote "No," and he would be sorry to do that which his conscience would compel him to do as an honest man. . . .

But Mr. Lincoln does not want to be held responsible for the Black Republican doctrine of no more Slave States. Farnsworth is the candidate of his party today in the Chicago District, and he made a speech in the last Congress in which he called upon

---

[23] When Texas was admitted to the Union in 1846, it was provided that additional States, not exceeding four in number, might be formed from it, with its consent. This condition was not availed of.

God to palsy his right arm if he ever voted for the admission of another Slave State, whether the people wanted it or not. Lovejoy is making speeches all over the State for Lincoln now, and taking ground against any more Slave States. Washburne, the Black Republican candidate for Congress in the Galena District, is making speeches in favor of this same Abolition platform, declaring no more Slave States. Why are men running for Congress in the northern districts, and taking that Abolition platform for their guide, when Mr. Lincoln does not want to be held to it down here in Egypt and in the center of the State, and objects to it so as to get votes here? Let me tell Mr. Lincoln that his party in the northern part of the State hold to that Abolition platform, and that if they do not in the south and in the center, they present the extraordinary spectacle of a "house divided against itself," and hence "cannot stand." I now bring down upon him the vengeance of his own Scriptural quotation, and give it a more appropriate application than he did, when I say to him that his party, Abolition in one end of the State and opposed to it in the other, is a house divided against itself, and cannot stand, and ought not to stand, for it attempts to cheat the American people out of their votes by disguising its sentiments. . . .

I was not born out West here. I was born away down in Yankee land. I was born in a valley in Vermont, with the high mountains around me. I love the old green mountains and valleys of Vermont, where I was born, and where I played in my childhood. I went up to visit them some seven or eight years ago, for the first time for twenty-odd years. When I got there they treated me very kindly. They invited me to the commencement of their college, placed me on the seats with their distinguished guests, and conferred upon me the degree of LL.D., in Latin (doctor of laws),—the same as they did Old Hickory, at Cambridge, many years ago; and I give you my word and honor I understand just as much of Latin as he did. When they got through conferring the honorary degree, they called upon me for a speech; and I got up, with my heart full and swelling with gratitude for their kindness, and I said to them, "My friends, Vermont is the most glorious spot on the face of this globe for a man to be born in, provided he emigrates when he is very young." I emigrated when I was very young. I came out here when I was a boy, and I found my mind liberalized, and my opinions enlarged, when I got on these broad prairies, with only the heavens to bound my vision, instead of having them circumscribed by the little narrow ridges that surrounded the valley where I was born.

Mr. Lincoln has framed another question, propounded it to me, and desired my answer. It is as follows: "If the slaveholding citizens of a United States Territory should need and demand Congressional legislation for the protection of their slave property in such Territory, would you, as a member of Congress, vote for or against such legislation?" I answer him that it is a fundamental article in the Democratic creed that there should be non-interference and non-intervention by Congress with slavery in the States or Territories. Mr. Lincoln could have found an answer to his question in the Cincinnati platform, if he had desired it. The Democratic party has always stood by that great principle of non-interference and non-intervention by Congress with slavery in the States and Territories alike, and I stand on that platform now.

Now, I desire to call your attention to the fact that Lincoln did not define his own position in his own question. How does he stand on that question? He put the question to me at Freeport whether or not I would vote to admit Kansas into the Union before she had 93,420 inhabitants. I answered him at once that, it having been decided that Kansas had now population enough for a Slave State, she had population enough for a Free State.

I answered the question unequivocally; and then I asked him whether he would vote for or against the admission of Kansas before she had 93,420 inhabitants, and he would not answer me. Today he has called attention to the fact that, in his opinion, my answer on that question was not quite plain enough, and yet he has not answered it himself. He now puts a question in relation to the Congressional interference in the

Territories to me. I answer him direct, and he has not answered the question himself. I ask you whether a man has any right, in common decency, to put questions in these public discussions, to his opponent, which he will not answer himself, when they are pressed home to him. I have asked him three times whether he would vote to admit Kansas whenever the people applied with a Constitution of their own making, and their own adoption, under circumstances that were fair, just, and unexceptionable; but I cannot get an answer from him. Nor will he answer the question which he put to me, and which I have just answered, in relation to Congressional interference in the Territories, by making a slave code there.

It is true that he goes on to answer the question by arguing that under the decision of the Supreme Court it is the duty of a man to vote for a slave code in the Territories. He says that it is his duty, under the decision that the court has made; and if he believes in that decision he would be a perjured man if he did not give the vote. I want to know whether he is not bound to a decision which is contrary to his opinions just as much as to one in accordance with his opinions. If the decision of the Supreme Court, the tribunal created by the Constitution to decide the question, is final and binding, is he not bound by it just as strongly as if he was for it instead of against it, originally? Is every man in this land allowed to resist decisions he does not like, and only support those that meet his approval? What are important courts worth, unless their decisions are binding on all good citizens? It is the fundamental principle of the judiciary that its decisions are final. It is created for that purpose; so that when you cannot agree among yourselves on a disputed point you appeal to the judicial tribunal, which steps in and decides for you, and that decision is then binding on every good citizen. It is the law of the land just as much with Mr. Lincoln against it as for it. And yet he says that if that decision is binding he is a perjured man if he does not vote for a slave code in the different Territories of this Union. Well, if you (turning to Mr. Lincoln) are not going to resist the decision, if you obey it, and do not intend to array mob law against the constituted authorities, then, according to your own statement, you will be a perjured man if you do not vote to establish slavery in these Territories. My doctrine is, that even taking Mr. Lincoln's view that the decision recognizes the right of a man to carry his slaves into the Territories of the United States if he pleases, yet after he gets there he needs affirmative law to make that right of any value. The same doctrine not only applies to slave property, but all other kinds of property. Chief Justice Taney[24] places it upon the ground that slave property is on an equal footing with other property. Suppose one of your merchants should move to Kansas and open a liquor store; he has a right to take groceries and liquors there; but the mode of selling them, and the circumstances under which they shall be sold, and all the remedies, must be prescribed by local legislation; and if that is unfriendly it will drive him out just as effectually as if there was a constitutional provision against the sale of liquor. So the absence of local legislation to encourage and support slave property in a Territory excludes it practically just as effectually as if there was a positive Constitutional provision against it. Hence, I assert that under the Dred Scott decision you cannot maintain slavery a day in a Territory where there is an unwilling people and unfriendly legislation. If the people are opposed to it, our right is a barren, worthless, useless right; and if they are for it, they will support and encourage it. We come right back, therefore, to the practical question, if the people of a Territory want slavery they will have it, and if they do not want it, you cannot force it on them. And this is the practical question, the great principle, upon which our institutions rest. I am willing to take the decision of the Supreme

---

[24] Roger B. Taney (pronounced Taw'ny) was the Chief Justice of the United States Supreme Court who wrote the decision that Dred Scott continued to be a slave after having resided in free territory.

Court as it was pronounced by that august tribunal, without stopping to inquire whether I would have decided that way or not. . . . In a government of laws, like ours, we must sustain the Constitution as our fathers made it, and maintain the rights of the States as they are guaranteed under the Constitution; and then we will have peace and harmony between the different States and sections of this glorious Union.

FOURTH JOINT DEBATE

Charleston, September 18, 1858

MR. LINCOLN'S SPEECH

Ladies and Gentlemen: It will be very difficult for an audience so large as this to hear distinctly what a speaker says, and consequently it is important that as profound silence be preserved as possible.

While I was at the hotel to-day, an elderly gentleman called upon me to know whether I was really in favor of producing perfect equality between the negroes and white people. While I had not proposed to myself on this occasion to say much on that subject, yet as the question was asked me, I thought I would occupy perhaps five minutes in saying something in regard to it. I will say then that I am not, nor ever have been, in favor of bringing about in any way the social and political equality of the white and black races; that I am not, nor ever have been, in favor of making voters or jurors of negroes, nor of qualifying them to hold office, nor to intermarry with white people; and I will say in addition to this that there is a physical difference between the white and black races which I believe will forever forbid the two races living together on terms of social and political equality. And inasmuch as they cannot so live, while they do remain together there must be the position of superior and inferior, and I, as much as any other man, am in favor of having the superior position assigned to the white race. I say upon this occasion I do not perceive that because the white man is to have the superior position, the negro should be denied everything. I do not understand that because I do not want a negro woman for a slave I must necessarily want her for a wife. My understanding is that I can just let her alone. I am now in my fiftieth year, and I certainly never had a black woman for either a slave or a wife. So it seems to me quite possible for us to get along without making either slaves or wives of negroes. . . . But as Judge Douglas and his friends seem to be in great apprehension that they might, if there were no law to keep them from it, I give the most solemn pledge that I will, to the very last, stand by the law of this State, which forbids the marrying of white people with negroes. I will add one further word, which is this: that I do not understand that there is any place where an alteration of the social and political relations of the negro and the white man can be made, except in the State Legislature,—not in the Congress of the United States; and as I do not really apprehend the approach of any such thing myself, and as Judge Douglas seems to be in constant horror that some such danger is rapidly approaching, I propose as the best means to prevent it, that the Judge be kept at home and placed in the State Legislature to fight the measure. I do not propose dwelling longer at this time on this subject.

SENATOR DOUGLAS'S SPEECH

Ladies and Gentlemen: I had supposed that we assembled here to-day for the purpose of a joint discussion between Mr. Lincoln and myself, upon the political questions that now agitate the whole country. The rule of such discussions is, that the opening speaker shall touch upon all the points he intends to discuss, in order that his opponent, in reply, shall have the opportunity of answering them. Let me ask you, what questions of public policy, relating to the welfare of this State or the Union, has Mr. Lincoln discussed before you? Mr. Lincoln simply contented himself at the outset by saying that he was not in favor of social and political equality between the white man and the negro, and did not desire the law so changed as to make the latter voters or eligible to office. I am glad that I have at last succeeded in getting an answer out of him upon this question of negro citizenship and eligibility to office, for I have been trying to bring him to the point on it ever since this canvass commenced. . . .

Fellow-citizens, I came here for the purpose of discussing the leading political topics which now agitate the country. I have no charges to make against Mr. Lincoln, none against Mr. Trumbull, and none against any man who is a candidate, except in repelling their assaults upon me. If Mr. Lincoln is a man of bad character, I leave you to find it out; if his votes in the past are not satisfactory, I leave others to ascertain the fact; if his course on the Mexican War was not in accordance with your notions of patriotism and fidelity to our own country as against a public enemy, I leave you to ascertain the fact. I have no assaults to make upon him, except to trace his course on the questions that now divide the country and engross so much of the people's attention. . . .

I canvassed the State that year from the time I returned home until the election[25] came off, and spoke in every county that I could reach during that period. In the northern part of the State I found Lincoln's ally, in the person of Fred Douglass's, the negro, preaching Abolition doctrines, while Lincoln was discussing the same principles down here, and Trumbull, a little farther down, was advocating the election of members to the Legislature who would act in concert with Lincoln's and Fred Douglass's friends. I witnessed an effort made at Chicago by Lincoln's then associates, and now supporters, to put Fred Douglass, the negro, on the stand at a Democratic meeting, to reply to the illustrious General Cass,[26] when he was addressing the people there. They had the same negro hunting me down, and they now have a negro traversing the northern counties of the State and speaking in behalf of Lincoln. Lincoln knows that when we were at Freeport in joint discussion there was a distinguished colored friend of his there then, who was on the stump for him, and who made a speech there the night before we spoke, and another the

---

[25] The State Legislative election of 1834.

[26] Lewis Cass, Michigan, Democrat, was Secretary of State under President Buchanan, but resigned when Buchanan refused to reinforce Major Anderson at Fort Sumter.

night after, a short distance from Freeport, in favor of Lincoln; and in order to show how much interest the colored brethren felt in the success of their brother Abe, I have with me here, and would read it if it would not occupy too much of my time, a speech made by Fred Douglass in Poughkeepsie, N. Y., a short time since, to a large convention, in which he conjures all the friends of negro equality and negro citizenship to rally as one man around Abraham Lincoln, the perfect embodiment of their principles, and by all means to defeat Stephen A. Douglas. . . .

And now I will explain to you what has been a mystery all over the State and Union,—the reason why Lincoln was nominated for the United States Senate by the Black Republican Convention. You know it has never been usual for any party, or any convention, to nominate a candidate for United States Senator. Probably this was the first time that such a thing was ever done. The Black Republican Convention had not been called for that purpose, but to nominate a State ticket, and every man was surprised, and many disgusted, when Lincoln was nominated. . . . He received the nomination unanimously, by a resolution declaring that Abraham Lincoln was "the first, last, and only choice" of the Republican party. How did this occur? Why, because they could not get Lincoln's friends to make another bargain with "rogues," unless the whole party would come up as one man and pledge their honor that they would stand by Lincoln first, last, and all the time, and that he should not be cheated by Lovejoy this time, as he was by Trumbull before. Thus, by passing this resolution, the Abolitionists are all for him, Lovejoy and Farnsworth[27] are canvassing for him, Giddings[28] is ready to come here in his behalf, and the negro speakers are already on the stump for him, and he is sure not to be cheated this time. He would not go into the arrangement until he got their bond for it, and Trumbull is compelled now to take the stump, get up false charges against me, and travel all over the State to try and elect Lincoln, in

---

[27] John F. Farnsworth, a Republican member of Congress from Illinois.

[28] Joshua R. Giddings, member of Congress from Ohio and prominent as an opponent of slavery.

order to keep Lincoln's friends quiet about the bargain in which Trumbull cheated them four years ago. You see, now, why it is that Lincoln and Trumbull are so mighty fond of each other. They have entered into a conspiracy to break me down by these assaults on my public character, in order to draw my attention from a fair exposure of the mode in which they attempted to Abolitionize the old Whig and the old Democratic parties, and lead them captive into the Abolition camp. . . .

["The party does not call itself Black Republican in the North."]

Sir, if you will get a copy of the paper published at Waukegan, fifty miles from Chicago, which advocates the election of Mr. Lincoln, and has his name flying at its mast-head, you will find that it declares that "this paper is devoted to the cause" of Black Republicanism. . . .

I am told that I have eight minutes more. I would like to talk to you an hour and a half longer, but I will make the best use I can of the remaining eight minutes. Mr. Lincoln said in his first remarks that he was not in favor of the social and political equality of the negro with the white man. Everywhere up north he had declared that he was not in favor of the social and political equality of the negro, but he would not say whether or not he was opposed to negroes voting, and negro citizenship. I want to know whether he is for or against negro citizenship. He declared his utter opposition to the Dred Scott decision, and advanced as a reason that the court had decided that it was not possible for a negro to be a citizen under the Constitution of the United States. If he is opposed to the Dred Scott decision for that reason, he must be in favor of conferring the right and privilege of citizenship upon the negro. I have been trying to get an answer from him on that point, but have never yet obtained one. . . .

MR. LINCOLN'S REJOINDER

Fellow-citizens: It follows as a matter of course that a half-hour answer to a speech of an hour and a half can be but a very hurried one. I shall only be able to touch upon a few of the points suggested by Judge Douglas, and give them a brief attention, while I shall have to totally omit others for the want of time.

Judge Douglas has said to you that he has not been able to get from me an answer to the question whether I am in favor of negro citizenship. So far as I know, the Judge never asked me the question before. He shall have no occasion to ever ask it again, for I tell him very frankly that I am not in favor of negro citizenship. This furnishes me an occasion for saying a few words upon the subject. I mentioned, in a certain speech of mine which has been printed, that the Supreme Court had decided that a negro could not possibly be made a citizen; and without saying what was my ground of complaint in regard to that, or whether I had any ground of complaint, Judge Douglas has from that thing manufactured nearly everything that he ever says about my disposition to produce an equality between the negroes and the white people. If anyone will read my speech, he will find I mentioned that as one of the points decided in the course of the Supreme Court opinions, but I did not state what objection I had to it. But Judge Douglas tells the people what my objection was, when I did not tell them myself. Now, my opinion is, that the different States have the power to make a negro a citizen under the Constitution of the United States, if they choose. The Dred Scott decision decides that they have not that power. If the State of Illinois had that power, I should be opposed to the exercise of it. That is all I have to say about it.

Judge Douglas has told me that he heard my speeches north, and my speeches south; that he had heard me at Ottawa and at Freeport in the north, and recently at Jonesboro in the south, and there was a very different cast of sentiment in the speeches made at the different points. I will not charge upon Judge Douglas that he wilfully misrepresents me, but I call upon every fair-minded man to take these speeches and read them, and I dare him to point out any difference between my speeches north and south. While I am here perhaps I ought to say a word, if I have the time, in regard to the latter portion of the Judge's speech, which was a sort of declamation in reference to my having said I entertained the belief that this Government would not endure, half slave and half free. I have said so, and I did not say it without what seemed to me to be good reasons. It perhaps would require more time than I have now to set forth these reasons in detail; but let me ask you a few questions. Have we ever had any peace on this slavery question? When are we to have peace upon it, if it is kept in the position it now occupies? How are we ever to have peace upon it? That is an important question. To be sure, if we will all stop, and allow Judge Douglas and his friends to march on in their present career until they plant the institution all over the nation, here, and wherever else our flag waves, and we acquiesce in it, there will be peace. But let me ask Judge Douglas how he is going to get the people to do that? They have been wrangling over this question for at least forty years. This was the cause of the agitation resulting in the Missouri Compromise; this produced the troubles at the annexation of Texas, in the acquisition of the territory acquired in the Mexican War. Again, this was the trouble which was quieted by the Compromise of 1850, when it was settled "forever," as both the great political parties declared in their National Conventions. That "forever" turned out to be just four years, when Judge Douglas himself reopened it. When is it likely to come to an end? He introduced the Nebraska bill in 1854 to put another end to the slavery agitation. He promised that it would finish it all up immediately, and he has never made a speech since, until he got into a quarrel with the President about the Lecompton Constitution,[29] in which he has not declared that we are just at the end of the slavery agitation. But in one speech, I think last winter, he did say that he didn't quite see when the end of the slavery agitation would come. Now he tells us again that it is all over, and the people of Kansas have voted down the Lecompton Constitution. How is it over? That was only one of the attempts at putting an end to the slavery agitation,—one of those "final settlements." Is Kansas in the

---

[29] Some citizens of Kansas Territory, in 1857, held a convention at Lecompton and formed a constitution, upon which the anti-slavery people refused to vote. Although adopted "with slavery," Congress accepted the Constitution; but it was not put into effect by the people of the territory.

Union? Has she formed a constitution that she is likely to come in under? Is not the slavery agitation still an open question in that Territory? Has the voting down of that constitution put an end to all the trouble? Is that more likely to settle it than every one of these previous attempts to settle the slavery agitation? Now, at this day in the history of the world, we can no more foretell where the end of this slavery agitation will be than we can see the end of the world itself. The Nebraska–Kansas bill[30] was introduced four years and a half ago, and if the agitation is ever to come to an end, we may say we are four years and a half nearer the end. So, too, we can say we are four years and a half nearer the end of the world; and we can just as clearly see the end of the world as we can see the end of this agitation. The Kansas settlement did not conclude it. If Kansas should sink to-day, and leave a great vacant space in the earth's surface, this vexed question would still be among us. I say, then, there is no way of putting an end to the slavery agitation amongst us, but to put it back upon the basis where our fathers placed it; no way but to keep it out of our new Territories,—to restrict it forever to the old States where it now exists. Then the public mind will rest in the belief that it is in the course of ultimate extinction. That is one way of putting an end to the slavery agitation.

The other way is for us to surrender, and let Judge Douglas and his friends have their way and plant slavery over all the States; cease speaking of it as in any way a wrong; regard slavery as one of the common matters of property, and speak of negroes as we do of our horses and cattle. But while it drives on in its state of progress as it is now driving, and as it has driven for the last five years, I have ventured the opinion, and I say to-day, that we will have no end to the slavery agitation until it takes one turn or the other. . . .

My colleague says he is willing to stand on his public record. By that he shall be tried; and if he had been able to

---

[30] In 1854, Congress passed an act to divide Nebraska into two Territories, leaving the people of each Territory to decide whether they would come into the Union as a slave or a free State. This was "squatter sovereignty."

discriminate between the exposure of a public act by the record, and a personal attack upon the individual, he would have discovered that there was nothing personal in my Chicago remarks, unless the condemnation of himself by his own public record is personal; and then you must judge who is most to blame for the torture his public record inflicts upon him: he for making, or I for reading it after it was made. As an individual I care very little about Judge Douglas one way or the other. It is his public acts with which I have to do, and if they condemn, disgrace, and consign him to oblivion, he has only himself, not me, to blame. . . .

FIFTH JOINT DEBATE

Galesburg, October 7, 1858

MR. DOUGLAS'S SPEECH

Ladies and Gentlemen: Four years ago I appeared before the people of Knox County[31] for the purpose of defending my political action upon the Compromise measures of 1850 and the passage of the Kansas-Nebraska bill. Those of you before me who were present then will remember that I vindicated myself for supporting those two measures by the fact that they rested upon the great fundamental principle that the people of each State and each Territory of this Union have the right, and ought to be permitted to exercise the right, of regulating their own domestic concerns in their own way, subject to no other limitation or restriction than that which the Constitution of the United States imposes upon them. I then called upon the people of Illinois to decide whether that principle of self-government was right or wrong. If it was and is right, then the Compromise measures of 1850 were right, and, consequently, the Kansas and Nebraska bill, based upon the same principle must necessarily have been right. . . .

["Good for Lincoln."]

Fellow-citizens, here you find men hurrahing for Lincoln, and saying that he did right, when in one part of the State he stood up for negro equality, and in another part, for political

---

[31] Galesburg is the county seat of Knox County, Illinois.

effect, discarded the doctrine, and declared that there always must be a superior and inferior race. Abolitionists up north are expected and required to vote for Lincoln, because he goes for the equality of the races, holding that by the Declaration of Independence the white man and the negro were created equal, and endowed by the divine law with that equality; and down south he tells the old Whigs, the Kentuckians, Virginians, and Tennesseans, that there is a physical difference in the races, making one superior and the other inferior, and that he is in favor of maintaining the superiority of the white race over the negro. Now, how can you reconcile those two positions of Mr. Lincoln? He is to be voted for in the south as a pro-slavery man, and he is to be voted for in the north as an Abolitionist. Up here he thinks it is all nonsense to talk about a difference between the races, and says that we must "discard all quibbling about this race and that race and the other race being inferior, and therefore they must be placed in an inferior position." Down south he makes this "quibble" about this race and that race and the other race being inferior as the creed of his party, and declares that the negro can never be elevated to the position of the white man. . . .

I tell you that this Chicago doctrine of Lincoln's—declaring that the negro and the white man are made equal by the Declaration of Independence and by Divine Providence—is a monstrous heresy. The signers of the Declaration of Independence never dreamed of the negro when they were writing that document. They referred to white men, to men of European birth and European descent, when they declared the equality of all men. I see a gentleman there in the crowd shaking his head. Let me remind him that when Thomas Jefferson wrote that document, he was the owner, and so continued until his death, of a large number of slaves. Did he intend to say in that Declaration, that his negro slaves, which he held and treated as property, were created his equals by divine law, and that he was violating the law of God every day of his life by holding them as slaves? It must be borne in mind that when that Declaration was put forth, every one of the thirteen Colonies were slaveholding Colonies, and every man who signed that instrument represented a slaveholding constituency. Recollect, also, that no one of them emancipated his slaves, much less put them on an equality with himself, after he signed the Declaration. On the contrary, they all continued to hold their negroes as slaves during the Revolutionary War. Now, do you believe—are you willing to have it said—that every man who signed the Declaration of Independence declared the negro his equal, and then was hypocrite enough to continue to hold him as a slave, in violation of what he believed to be the divine law? And yet when you say that the Declaration of Independence includes the negro, you charge the signers of it with hypocrisy.

I say to you, frankly, that in my opinion, this Government was made by our fathers on the white basis. It was made by white men for the benefit of white men and their posterity forever, and was intended to be administered by white men in all time to come. But while I hold that under our Constitution and political system the negro is not a citizen, cannot be a citizen, and ought not to be a citizen, it does not follow by any means that he should be a slave. On the contrary, it does follow that the negro, as an inferior race, ought to possess every right, every privilege, every immunity which he can safely exercise, consistent with the safety of the society in which he lives. Humanity requires, and Christianity commands, that you shall extend to every inferior being, and every dependent being, all the privileges, immunities, and advantages which can be granted to them, consistent with the safety of society. If you ask me the nature and extent of these privileges, I answer that that is a question which the people of each State must decide for themselves. Illinois has decided that question for herself. We have said that in this State the negro shall not be a slave, nor shall he be a citizen. Kentucky holds a different doctrine. New York holds one different from either, and Maine one different from all. Virginia, in her policy on this question, differs in many respects from the others, and so on, until there are hardly two States whose policy is exactly alike in regard to the relation of the white man and the negro. Nor can you reconcile them and make them alike. Each State must do as it pleases. Illinois had as much right to adopt the policy which we have on that subject as Kentucky had to adopt a different policy. The great principle of this Government is, that each State has the right to do as it pleases on all these questions, and no other State or power on earth has the right to interfere with us, or complain of us merely because our system differs from theirs. In the Compromise measures of 1850, Mr. Clay declared that this great principle ought to exist in the Territories as well as in the States, and I reasserted his doctrine in the Kansas and Nebraska bill in 1854.

But Mr. Lincoln cannot be made to understand, and those who are determined to vote for him, no matter whether he is a pro-slavery man in the South and a negro equality advocate in the North, cannot be made to understand how it is that in a Territory the people can do as they please on the slavery question under the Dred Scott decision. Let us see whether I cannot explain it to the satisfaction of all impartial men. Chief Justice Taney has said in his opinion in the Dred Scott case, that a negro slave being property, stands on an equal footing with other property, and that the owner may carry them into United States territory the same as he does other property. Suppose any two of you, neighbors, should conclude to go to Kansas, one carrying $100,000 worth of negro slaves, and the other $100,000 worth of mixed merchandise, including quantities of liquors. You both agree that under that decision you may carry your property to Kansas. But when you get there, the merchant who is possessed of the liquors is met by the Maine liquor law, which prohibits the sale or use of his property, and the owner of the slaves is met by equally unfriendly legislation, which makes his property worthless after he gets it there. What is the right to carry your property into the Territory worth to either, when unfriendly legislation in the Territory renders it worthless after you get it there. The slaveholder when he gets his slaves there finds that there is no local law to protect him in holding them, no slave code, no police regulation maintaining and supporting him in his right; and he discovers at once that the absence of such friendly legislation excludes his property from the Territory, just as irresistibly as if there was a positive Constitutional prohibition excluding it. Thus you find it is with any kind of property in a Territory, it depends for its protection on the local and municipal law. If the people of a Territory want slavery, they make friendly legislation to introduce it, but if they do not want it, they withhold all protection from it, and then it cannot exist there. Such was the view taken on the subject by different Southern men when the Nebraska bill passed. See the speech of Mr. Orr,[32] of South Carolina, the present Speaker of the House of Representatives of Congress, made at that time, and there you will find this whole doctrine argued out at full length. Read the speeches of other Southern Congressmen, Senators and Representatives, made in 1854, and you will find that they took the same view of the subject as Mr. Orr,—that slavery could never be forced on a people who did not want it. I hold that in this country there is no power on the face of the globe that can force any institution on an unwilling people. The great fundamental principle of our Government is that the people of each State and each Territory shall be left perfectly free to decide for themselves what shall be the nature and character of their institutions. When this Government was made, it was based on that principle. At the time of its formation there were twelve slaveholding States and one Free State in this Union. Suppose this doctrine of Mr. Lincoln and the Republicans, of uniformity of laws of all the States on the subject of slavery, had prevailed; suppose Mr. Lincoln himself had been a member of the Convention which framed the Constitution, and that he had risen in that august body, and addressing the Father of his Country, had said, as he did at Springfield:—

A house divided against itself cannot stand. I believe this Government cannot endure permanently, half slave and half free. I do not expect the Union to be dissolved, I do

---

[32] J. L. Orr of South Carolina, a Democrat, was a devoted friend of the Union and opposed to both nullification and secession.

not expect the house to fall, but I do expect it will cease
to be divided. It will become all one thing or all the other.

What do you think would have been the result? Suppose he
had made that convention believe that doctrine, and they had
acted upon it, what do you think would have been the result?
Do you believe that the one Free State would have outvoted the
twelve slaveholding States, and thus abolish slavery? On the contrary, would not the twelve slaveholding States have outvoted
the one Free State, and under his doctrine have fastened slavery
by an irrevocable constitutional provision upon every inch of the
American Republic? Thus you see that the doctrine he now
advocates, if proclaimed at the beginning of the Government,
would have established slavery everywhere throughout the
American Continent; and are you willing, now that we have the
majority section, to exercise a power which we never would
have submitted to when we were in the minority? If the
Southern States had attempted to control our institutions, and
make the States all slave when they had the power, I ask, would
you have submitted to it? If you would not, are you willing, now
that we have become the strongest, under that great principle of
self-government that allows each State to do as it pleases, to
attempt to control the Southern institutions? Then, my friends,
I say to you that there is but one path of peace in this Republic,
and that is to administer this Government as our fathers made
it, divided into Free and Slave States, allowing each State to
decide for itself whether it wants slavery or not. If Illinois will
settle the slavery question for herself, and mind her own business,
and let her neighbors alone, we will be at peace with Kentucky
and every other Southern State. If every other State in the Union
will do the same, there will be peace between the North and the
South, and in the whole Union.

MR. LINCOLN'S REPLY

The Judge has alluded to the Declaration of Independence,
and insisted that negroes are not included in that Declaration;
and that it is a slander upon the framers of that instrument to

suppose that negroes were meant therein; and he asks you: Is it possible to believe that Mr. Jefferson, who penned the immortal paper, could have supposed himself applying the language of that instrument to the negro race, and yet held a portion of that race in slavery? Would he not at once have freed them? I only have to remark upon this part of the Judge's speech (and that, too, very briefly, for I shall not detain myself, or you, upon that point for any great length of time), that I believe the entire records of the world, from the date of the Declaration of Independence up to within three years ago, may be searched in vain for one single affirmation, from one single man, that the negro was not included in the Declaration of Independence; I think I may defy Judge Douglas to show that he ever said so, that Washington ever said so, that any President ever said so, that any member of Congress ever said so, or that any living man upon the whole earth ever said so, until the necessities of the present policy of the Democratic party, in regard to slavery, had to invent that affirmation. And I will remind Judge Douglas and this audience that while Mr. Jefferson was the owner of slaves, as undoubtedly he was, in speaking upon this very subject he used the strong language that "he trembled for his country when he remembered that God was just;" and I will offer the highest premium in my power to Judge Douglas if he will show that he, in all his life, ever uttered a sentiment at all akin to that of Jefferson. . . .

Now a few words in regard to these extracts from speeches of mine, which Judge Douglas has read to you, and which he supposes are in very great contrast to each other. Those speeches have been before the public for a considerable time, and if they have any inconsistency in them, if there is any conflict in them, the public have been able to detect it. When the Judge says, in speaking on this subject, that I make speeches of one sort for the people of the northern end of the State, and of a different sort for the southern people, he assumes that I do not understand that my speeches will be put in print and read North and South. I knew all the while that the speech that I made at Chicago, and the one I made at Jonesboro and the one at Charleston, would all be put in print, and all the reading and intelligent men in the community would see them and know all about my opinions. And I have not supposed, and do not now suppose, that there is any conflict whatever between them. But the Judge will have it that if we do not confess that there is a sort of inequality between the white and black races, which justifies us in making them slaves, we must then insist that there is a degree of equality that requires us to make them our wives. Now, I have all the while taken a broad distinction in regard to that matter; and that is all there is in these different speeches which he arrays here; and the entire reading of either of the speeches will show that that distinction was made. Perhaps by taking two parts of the same speech he could have got up as much of a conflict as the one he has found. I have all the while maintained that in so far as it should be insisted that there was an equality between the white and black races that should produce a perfect social and political equality, it was an impossibility. This you have seen in my printed speeches, and with it I have said, that in their right to "life, liberty, and the pursuit of happiness," as proclaimed in that old Declaration, the inferior races are our equals. And these declarations I have constantly made in reference to the abstract moral question, to contemplate and consider when we are legislating about any new country which is not already cursed with the actual presence of the evil,—slavery. I have never manifested any impatience with the necessities that spring from the actual existence of slavery amongst us where it does already exist; but I have insisted that, in legislating for new countries where it does not exist, there is no just rule other than that of moral and abstract right! With reference to those new countries, those maxims as to the right of a people to "life, liberty, and the pursuit of happiness," were the just rules to be constantly referred to. There is no misunderstanding this, except by men interested to misunderstand it. I take it that I have to address an intelligent and reading community, who will peruse what I say, weigh it, and then judge whether I advance improper or unsound views, or whether I advance hypocritical, and deceptive, and contrary views in different portions of the country. I believe myself to be guilty of no such thing as the latter, though of course, I cannot claim that I am entirely free from all error in the opinions I advance.

The Judge has also detained us a while in regard to the distinction between his party and our party. His he assumes to be a national party,—ours a sectional one. He does this in asking the question whether this country has any interest in the maintenance of the Republican party. He assumes that our party is altogether sectional,—that the party to which he adheres is national; and the argument is, that no party can be a rightful party—can be based upon rightful principles— unless it can announce its principles everywhere. I presume that Judge Douglas could not go into Russia and announce the doctrine of our national Democracy; he could not denounce the doctrine of kings and emperors and monarchies in Russia; and it may be true of this country, that in some places we may not be able to proclaim a doctrine as clearly true as the truth of Democracy, because there is a section so directly opposed to it that they will not tolerate us in doing so. Is it the true test of the soundness of a doctrine that in some places people won't let you proclaim it? Is that the way to test the truth of any doctrine? Why, I understood that one time the people of Chicago would not let Judge Douglas preach a certain favorite doctrine of his. I commend to his consideration the question, whether he takes that as a test of the unsoundness of what he wanted to preach. . . .

We have a Republican State platform, laid down in Springfield, in June last, stating our position all the way through on the questions before the country. We are now far advanced in this canvass. Judge Douglas and I have made per- haps forty speeches apiece, and we have now for the fifth time met face to face in debate, and up to this day I have not found either Judge Douglas or any friend of his taking hold of the Republican platform, or laying his finger upon anything in it that is wrong. I ask you all to recollect that. Judge Douglas turns away from the platform of principles to the fact that he can find people somewhere who will not allow us to announce those principles. If he had great confidence that our principles were wrong, he would take hold of them and demonstrate them to be wrong. But he does not do so. The only evidence he has of their being wrong is in the fact that there are people who won't allow us to preach them. I ask again, is that the way to test the soundness of a doctrine?

I ask his attention also to the fact that by the rule of nationality he is himself fast becoming sectional. I ask his attention to the fact that his speeches would not go as current now south of the Ohio river as they have formerly gone there. I ask his attention to the fact that he felicitates himself to-day that all the Democrats of the Free States are agreeing with him, while he omits to tell us that the Democrats of any Slave State agree with him. If he has not thought of this, I commend to his consideration the evidence in his own declaration, on this day, of his becoming sectional too. I see it rapidly approaching. Whatever may be the result of this ephemeral contest between Judge Douglas and myself, I see the day rapidly approaching when his pill of sectionalism, which he has been thrusting down the throats of Republicans for years past, will be crowded down his own throat.

Now, in regard to what Judge Douglas said (in the beginning of his speech) about the Compromise of 1850 containing the principle of the Nebraska bill, although I have often presented my views upon that subject, yet as I have not done so in this canvass, I will, if you please, detain you a little with them. I have always maintained, so far as I was able, that there was nothing of the principle of the Nebraska bill in the Compromise of 1850 at all,—nothing whatever. Where can you find the principle of the Nebraska bill in the Compromise? If anywhere, in the two pieces of the Compromise organizing the Territories of New Mexico and Utah. It was expressly provided in these two Acts, that, when they came to be admitted into the Union, they should be admitted with or without slavery, as they should choose by their own constitutions. Nothing was said in either of those Acts as to what was to be done in relation to slavery during the territorial existence of those Territories, while Henry Clay constantly made the declaration (Judge Douglas recognizing him as a leader) that, in his opinion, the old Mexican laws would control that question during the territorial existence, and that these old Mexican laws excluded slavery. How can that be used as a principle for declaring that during the territorial existence as well as at the time of framing the Constitution, the people, if you please, might have slaves if they wanted them? I am not discussing the question whether it is right or wrong; but how are the New Mexican and Utah laws patterns for the Nebraska bill? I maintain that the organization of Utah and New Mexico did not establish a general principle at all. It had no feature of establishing a general principle. The Acts to which I have referred were a part of a general system of Compromises. They did not lay down what was proposed as a regular policy for the Territories, only an agreement in this particular case to do in that way, because other things were done that were to be a compensation for it. They were allowed to come in in that shape, because in another way it was paid for,—considering that as a part of that system of measures called the Compromise of 1850, which finally included half a dozen Acts. It included the admission of California as a Free State, which was kept out of the Union for a half a year because it had formed a free Constitution. It included the settlement of the boundary of Texas, which had been undefined before, which was in itself a slavery question; for if you pushed the line farther west, you made Texas larger, and made more slave territory; while, if you drew the line toward the east, you narrowed the boundary and diminished the domain of slavery, and by so much increased free territory. It included the abolition of the slave trade in the District of Columbia. It included the passage of a new Fugitive Slave law. All these things were put together, and though passed in separate Acts, were nevertheless, in legislation (as the speeches at the time will show), made to depend upon each other. Each got votes, with the understanding that the other measures were to pass, and by this system of compromise in that series of measures, those two bills—the New Mexico and

Utah bills—were passed; and I say for that reason they could not be taken as models, framed upon their own intrinsic principle, for all future Territories. And I have the evidence of this in the fact that Judge Douglas, a year afterward, or more than a year afterward, perhaps, when he first introduced bills for the purpose of framing new Territories, did not attempt to follow these bills of New Mexico and Utah; and even when he introduced this Nebraska bill, I think you will discover that he did not exactly follow them. But I do not wish to dwell at great length upon this branch of the discussion. My own opinion is, that a thorough investigation will show most plainly that the New Mexico and Utah bills were part of a system of compromise, and not designed as patterns for future Territorial legislation; and that this Nebraska bill did not follow them as a pattern at all. . . .

While we were at Freeport, in one of these joint discussions, I answered certain interrogatories which Judge Douglas had propounded to me, and then in turn propounded some to him which he in a sort of way answered. The third one of these interrogatories I have with me and wish now to make some comments upon it. It was in these words: "If the Supreme Court of the United States shall decide that the States cannot exclude slavery from their limits, are you in favor of acquiescing in, adhering to, and following such decision, as a rule of political action?"

To this interrogatory Judge Douglas made no answer in any just sense of the word. He contented himself with sneering at the thought that it was possible for the Supreme Court ever to make such a decision. He sneered at me for propounding the interrogatory. I had not propounded it without some reflection, and I wish now to address to this audience some remarks upon it.

In the second clause of the sixth article, I believe it is, of the Constitution of the United States, we find the following language: "This Constitution and the laws of the United States which shall be made in pursuance thereof; and all treaties made, or which shall be made, under the authority of the United

States, shall be the supreme law of the land; and the judges in every State shall be bound thereby, anything in the Constitution or laws of any State to the contrary, notwithstanding."

The essence of the Dred Scott case is compressed into the sentence which I will now read: "Now, as we have already said in an earlier part of this opinion, upon a different point, the right of property in a slave is distinctly and expressly affirmed in the Constitution." I repeat it; "The right of property in a slave is distinctly and expressly affirmed in the Constitution!" What is it to be "affirmed" in the Constitution? Made firm in the Constitution,—so made that it cannot be separated from the Constitution without breaking the Constitution; durable as the Constitution, and part of the Constitution. Now, remembering the provision of the Constitution which I have read; affirming that that instrument is the supreme law of the land; that the judges of every State shall be bound by it, any law or Constitution of any State to the contrary, notwithstanding; that the right of property in a slave is affirmed in that Constitution, is made, formed into, and cannot be separated from it without breaking it; durable as the instrument; part of the instrument;—what follows as a short and even syllogistic argument from it? I think it follows, and I submit to the consideration of men capable of arguing, whether as I state it in syllogistic form the argument has any fault in it:

Nothing in the Constitution or laws of any State can destroy a right distinctly and expressly affirmed in the Constitution of the United States.

The right of property in a slave is distinctly and expressly affirmed in the Constitution of the United States.

Therefore, nothing in the Constitution or laws of any State can destroy the right of property in a slave.

I believe that no fault can be pointed out in that argument; assuming the truth of the premises, the conclusion, so far as I have capacity at all to understand it, follows inevitably. There is a fault in it, as I think, but the fault is not in the reasoning; but the falsehood in fact is a fault of the premises. I believe that the right of property in a slave is not distinctly and expressly affirmed in the Constitution, and Judge Douglas thinks it is. I believe that the Supreme Court and the advocates of that decision may search in vain for the place in the Constitution where the right of a slave is distinctly and expressly affirmed. I say, therefore, that I think one of the premises is not true in fact. But it is true with Judge Douglas. It is true with the Supreme Court who pronounced it. They are estopped from denying it, and being estopped from denying it the conclusion follows that, the Constitution of the United States being the supreme law, no constitution or law can interfere with it. It being affirmed in the decision that the right of property in a slave is distinctly and expressly affirmed in the Constitution, the conclusion inevitably follows that no State law or constitution can destroy that right. I then say to Judge Douglas and to all others, that I think it will take a better answer than a sneer to show that those who have said that the right of property in a slave is distinctly and expressly affirmed in the Constitution, are not prepared to show that no constitution or law can destroy that right. . . .

I proposed to Judge Douglas another interrogatory, which was correlative to that: "Are you in favor of acquiring additional territory, in disregard of how it may affect us upon the slavery question?" Judge Douglas answered,—that is, in his own way he answered it. I believe that, although he took a good many words to answer it, it was a little more fully answered than any other. The substance of his answer was, that this country would continue to expand; that it would need additional territory; that it was as absurd to suppose that we could continue upon our present territory, enlarging in population as we are, as it would be to hoop a boy twelve years of age, and expect him to grow to man's size without bursting the hoops. I believe it was something like that. Consequently, he was in favor of the acquisition of further territory, as fast as we might need it, in disregard of how it might affect the slavery question. I do not say this as giving his exact language, but he said so substantially; and he would leave the question of slavery where the territory was acquired to be settled by the people of the acquired territory. ["That's the doctrine."] Maybe it is; let us consider that for a while. This will probably, in the run of things, become one of the concrete manifestations of this slavery question. If Judge Douglas's policy upon this question succeeds, and gets fairly settled down, until all opposition is crushed out, the next thing will be a grab for the territory of poor Mexico, an invasion of the rich lands of South America, then the adjoining islands will follow, each one of which promises additional slave-fields. And this question is to be left to the people of those countries for settlement. When we shall get Mexico, I don't know whether the Judge will be in favor of the Mexican people that we get with it settling that question for themselves and all others; because we know the Judge has a great horror for mongrels, and I understand that the people of Mexico are most decidedly a race of mongrels. I understand that there is not more than one person there out of eight who is pure white, and I suppose from the Judge's previous declaration that when we get Mexico or any considerable portion of it, that he will be in favor of these mongrels settling the question, which would bring him somewhat into collusion with his horror of an inferior race.

It is to be remembered, though, that this power of acquiring additional territory is a power confided to the President and Senate of the United States. It is a power not under the control of the representatives of the people any further than they, the President and the Senate, can be considered the representatives of the people. Let me illustrate that by a case we have in our history. When we acquired the territory from Mexico in the Mexican War, the House of Representatives, composed of the immediate representatives of the people, all the time insisted that the territory thus to be acquired should be brought in upon condition that slavery should be forever prohibited therein, upon the terms and in the language that slavery had been prohibited from coming into this country. This was insisted upon constantly and never failed to call forth an assurance that any territory thus acquired should have that prohibition in it, so far as the House of Representatives was concerned. But at last the

President and Senate acquired the territory without asking the House of Representatives anything about it, and took it without that prohibition. They have the power of acquiring territory without the immediate representatives of the people being called upon to say anything about it and thus furnishing a very apt and powerful means of bringing new territory into the Union, and, when it is once brought into the country, involving us anew in this slavery agitation. It is, therefore, as I think, a very important question for the consideration of the American people, whether the policy of bringing in additional territory, without considering at all how it will operate upon the safety of the Union in reference to this one great disturbing element in our national politics, shall be adopted as the policy of the country. You will bear in mind that it is to be acquired, according to the Judge's view, as fast as it is needed, and the indefinite part of this proposition is that we have only Judge Douglas and his class of men to decide how fast it is needed. We have no clear and certain way of determining or demonstrating how fast territory is needed by the necessities of the country. Whoever wants to go out filibustering, then, thinks that more territory is needed. Whoever wants wider slave-fields, feels sure that some additional territory is needed as slave territory. Then it is as easy to show the necessity of additional slave territory as it is to assert anything that is incapable of absolute demonstration. Whatever motive a man or a set of men may have for making annexation of property or territory, it is very easy to assert, but much less easy to disprove, that it is necessary for the wants of the country. . . .

MR. DOUGLAS'S REPLY

Mr. Lincoln asserts to-day, as he did at Chicago, that the negro was included in that clause of the Declaration of Independence which says that all men were created equal, and endowed by the Creator with certain inalienable rights, among which are life, liberty, and the pursuit of happiness. If the negro was made his equal and mine, if that equality was established by divine law, and was the negro's inalienable right, how came he to say at Charleston to the Kentuckians

residing in that section of our State, that the negro was phys-
ically inferior to the white man, belonged to an inferior race,
and he was for keeping him always in that inferior condition.
I wish you to bear these things in mind. At Charleston he said
that the negro belonged to an inferior race, and that he was
for keeping him in that inferior condition. There he gave the
people to understand that there was no moral question
involved, because the inferiority being established it was only
a question of degree, and not a question of right; here, to-day,
instead of making it a question of degree, he makes it a moral
question, says that it is a great crime to hold the negro in that
inferior condition. ["He's right."] Is he right now, or was he
right in Charleston? ["Both."] He is right then, sir, in your
estimation, not because he is consistent, but because he can
trim his principles any way, in any section, so as to secure voters. All I desire of him is that he will declare the same principles in the South that he does in the North. . . .

He complains because I did not go into an argument
reviewing Chief Justice Taney's opinion, and the other opinions of the different judges, to determine whether their reasoning is right or wrong on the questions of law. What use would
that be? He wants to take an appeal from the Supreme Court
to this meeting, to determine whether the questions of law
were decided properly. He is going to appeal from the
Supreme Court of the United States to every town meeting, in
the hope that he can excite a prejudice against that Court, and
on the wave of that prejudice ride into the Senate of the
United States, when he could not get there on his own principles or his own merits. Suppose he should succeed in getting
into the Senate of the United States, what then will he have to
do with the decision of the Supreme Court in the Dred Scott
case? Can he reverse that decision when he gets there? Can he
act upon it? Has the Senate any right to reverse it or revise it?
He will not pretend that it has. Then why drag the matter into
this contest, unless for the purpose of making a false issue, by
which he can direct public attention from the real issue. . .

SIXTH JOINT DEBATE

Quincy, October 13, 1858

MR. LINCOLN'S SPEECH

Ladies and Gentlemen: I have had no immediate conference with Judge Douglas, but I will venture to say that he and I will perfectly agree that your entire silence, both when I speak and when he speaks, will be most agreeable to us. . . .

When the Judge says he wouldn't have believed of Abraham Lincoln that he would have made such an attempt as that, he reminds me of the fact that he entered upon this canvass with the purpose to treat me courteously; that touched me somewhat. It sets me to thinking. I was aware, when it was first agreed that Judge Douglas and I were to have these seven joint discussions, that they were the successive acts of a drama,—perhaps I should say, to be enacted, not merely in the face of audiences like this, but in the face of the nation, and to some extent, by my relation to him, and not from anything in myself, in the face of the world; and I am anxious that they should be conducted with dignity and in the good temper which would be befitting the vast audience before which it was conducted. . . .

We have in this nation this element of domestic slavery. It is a matter of absolute certainty that it is a disturbing element. It is the opinion of all the great men who have expressed an opinion upon it, that it is a dangerous element. We keep up a controversy in regard to it. That controversy necessarily springs from difference of opinion; and if we can learn

exactly—can reduce to the lowest elements—what this difference of opinion is, we shall perhaps be better prepared for
discussing the different systems of policy that we would propose in regard to that disturbing element. I suggest that the
difference of opinion, reduced to its lowest terms, is no other
than the difference between the men who think slavery a
wrong and those who do not think it wrong. The Republican
party thinks it wrong; we think it is a moral, a social, and a
political wrong. We think it is a wrong not confining itself
merely to the persons or the States where it exists, but that it
is a wrong in its tendency, to say the least, that extends itself
to the existence of the whole nation. Because we think it
wrong, we propose a course of policy that shall deal with it
as a wrong. We deal with it as with any other wrong, in so
far as we can prevent its growing any larger, and so deal with
it that in the run of time there may be some promise of an
end to it. We have a due regard to the actual presence of it
amongst us, and the difficulties of getting rid of it in any satisfactory way, and all the constitutional obligations thrown
about it. I suppose that in reference both to its actual existence in the nation, and to our constitutional obligations, we
have no right at all to disturb it in the States where it exists,
and we profess that we have no more inclination to disturb it
than we have the right to do it. We go further than that; we
don't propose to disturb it where, in one instance, we think
the Constitution would permit us. We think the Constitution
would permit us to disturb it in the District of Columbia.
Still, we do not propose to do that, unless it should be in
terms which I don't suppose the nation is very likely soon to
agree to,—the terms of making the emancipation gradual,
and compensating the unwilling owners. Where we suppose
we have the constitutional right, we restrain ourselves in reference to the actual existence of the institution and the difficulties thrown about it. We also oppose it as an evil, so far
as it seeks to spread itself. We insist on the policy that shall
restrict it to its present limits. We don't suppose that in doing

this we violate anything due to the actual presence of the institution, or anything due to the constitutional guarantees thrown around it.

We oppose the Dred Scott decision in a certain way, upon which I ought perhaps to address you a few words. We do not propose that when Dred Scott has been decided to be a slave by the court, we, as a mob, will decide him to be free. We do not propose that, when any other one, or one thousand, shall be decided by that court to be slaves, we will in any violent way disturb the rights of property thus settled; but we nevertheless do oppose that decision as a political rule which shall be binding on the voter to vote for nobody who thinks it wrong, which shall be binding on the members of Congress or the President to favor no measure that does not actually concur with the principles of that decision. We do not propose to be bound by it as a political rule in that way, because we think it lays the foundation, not merely of enlarging and spreading out what we consider an evil, but it lays the foundation for spreading that evil into the States themselves. We propose so resisting it as to have it reversed if we can, and a new judicial rule established upon this subject. I will add this, that if there be any man who does not believe that slavery is wrong in the three aspects which I have mentioned, or in any one of them, that man is misplaced, and ought to leave us. While, on the other hand, if there be any man in the Republican party who is impatient over the necessity springing from its actual presence, and is impatient of the constitutional guarantees thrown around it, and would act in disregard of these, he too is misplaced, standing with us. He will find his place somewhere else; for we have a due regard, so far as we are capable of understanding them, for all these things. This, gentlemen, as well as I can give it, is a plain statement of our principles in their enormity.

I will say now that there is a sentiment in the country contrary to me,—a sentiment which holds that slavery is not wrong, and therefore it goes for the policy that does not propose dealing with it as a wrong. That policy is the Democratic policy, and that sentiment is the Democratic sentiment. If there be a doubt in the mind of any one of this vast audience that this is really the central idea of the Democratic party in relation to this subject, I ask him to bear with me while I state a few things tending, as I think, to prove that proposition. In the first place, the leading man—I think I may do my friend Judge Douglas the honor of calling him such—advocating the present Democratic policy, never himself says it is wrong. He has the high distinction, so far as I know, of never having said slavery is either right or wrong. Almost everybody else says one or the other, but the Judge never does. If there be a man in the Democratic party who thinks it is wrong, and yet clings to that party, suggest to him in the first place, that his leader don't talk as he does, for he never says that it is wrong. In the second place, I suggest to him, that if he will examine the policy proposed to be carried forward, he will find that he carefully excludes the idea that there is anything wrong in it. If you will examine the arguments that are made on it, you will find that every one carefully excludes the idea that there is anything wrong in slavery. Perhaps that Democrat who says that he is as much opposed to slavery as I am, will tell me that I am wrong about this. I wish him to examine his own course in regard to this matter a moment, and then see if his opinion will not be changed a little. You say it is wrong; but don't you constantly object to anybody else saying so? Do you not constantly argue that this is not the right place to oppose it? You say it must not be opposed in the Free States, because slavery is not here; it must not be opposed in the Slave States, because it is there; it must not be opposed in politics, because that will make a fuss; it must not be opposed in the pulpit, because it is not religion. Then where is the place to oppose it? There is no suitable place to oppose it. There is no place in the country to oppose this evil overspreading the continent, which you say yourself is coming. Frank Blair[33] and Gratz Brown[34] tried to get up a system of gradual emancipation in Missouri, had an election in August, and got beat, and you, Mr. Democrat, threw up your hat and hallooed "hurrah for Democracy." So I say again, that in regard to the arguments that are made, when Judge Douglas says he "don't care whether slavery is voted up or voted down," whether he means that as an individual expression of sentiment, or only as a sort of statement of his views on national policy, it is alike true to say that he can thus argue logically if he don't see anything wrong in it; but he cannot say so logically if he admits that slavery is wrong. He cannot say that he would as soon see a wrong voted up as voted down. When Judge Douglas says that whoever or whatever community wants slaves, they have a right to have them, he is perfectly logical, if there is nothing wrong in the institution; but if you admit that it is wrong, he cannot logically say that anybody has a right to do wrong. When he says that slave property and horse and hog property are alike to be allowed to go into the Territories, upon the principles of equality, he is reasoning truly, if there is no difference between them as property; but if the one is property held rightfully, and the other is wrong, then there is no equality between the right and wrong; so that, turn it in any way you can, in all the arguments sustaining the Democratic policy, and in that policy itself, there is a carefully studied exclusion of the idea that there is anything wrong in slavery. Let us understand this. I am not, just here, trying to prove that we are right, and they are wrong. I have

---

[33] Francis P. Blair, Jr. of Missouri was a member of Congress at this time. He later was a Major General in the Union Army and was the Democratic candidate for Vice-President in 1868.

[34] B. Gratz Brown at this time was a member of the State Legislature of Missouri. He served in the Union army in the civil war, was United States Senator from Missouri 1863–7, became Governor of Missouri in 1871, and was candidate for Vice-President on the ticket with Horace Greeley in 1872.

been stating where we and they stand, and trying to show what is the real difference between us; and I now say that whenever we can get the question distinctly stated, can get all these men who believe that slavery is in some of these respects wrong, to stand and act with us in treating it as a wrong,—then, and not till then, I think we will in some way come to an end of this slavery agitation.

MR. DOUGLAS'S REPLY

Mr. Lincoln pretends that after I had so quoted those resolutions[35] he discovered that they had never been adopted at Springfield. . . .

I will now show you that I stated with entire fairness, as soon as it was made known to me, that there was a mistake about the spot where the resolutions had been adopted, although their truthfulness, as a declaration of the principles of the Republican party, had not and could not be questioned. I did not wait for Lincoln to point out the mistake, but the moment I discovered it, I made a speech, and published it to the world, correcting the error. I corrected it myself, as a gentleman and an honest man, and as I always feel proud to do when I have made a mistake. I wish Mr. Lincoln could show that he has acted with equal fairness, and truthfulness, when I have convinced him that he has been mistaken. I will give you an illustration to show you how he acts in a similar case: In a speech at Springfield, he charged Chief Justice Taney and his associates, President Pierce, President Buchanan, and myself, with having entered into a conspiracy at the time the Nebraska bill was introduced, by which the Dred Scott decision was to be made by the Supreme Court, in order to carry slavery everywhere under the Constitution. I called his attention to the fact that at the time alluded to, to wit, the introduction of the Nebraska bill, it was not possible that such a conspiracy could have been entered into, for the reason that the Dred Scott case had never

---

[35] Referring to the Resolutions given on pages 3–4.

been taken before the Supreme Court, and was not taken before it for a year after; and I asked him to take back that charge. Did he do it? I showed him that it was impossible that the charge could be true; I proved it by the record: and I then called upon him to retract his false charge. What was his answer? Instead of coming out like an honest man and doing so, he reiterated the charge, and said that if the case had not gone up to the Supreme Court from the courts of Missouri at the time he charged that the Judges of the Supreme Court entered into the conspiracy, yet that there was an understanding with the Democratic owners of Dred Scott that they would take it up. I have since asked him who the Democratic owners of Dred Scott were, but he could not tell, and why? Because there were no such Democratic owners in existence. Dred Scott at the time was owned by the Rev. Dr. Chaffee, an Abolition member of Congress, of Springfield, Massachusetts, in right of his wife. He was owned by one of Lincoln's friends, and not by Democrats at all; his case was conducted in court by Abolition lawyers, so that both the prosecution and the defense were in the hands of the Abolition political friends of Mr. Lincoln. Notwithstanding I thus proved by the record that his charge against the Supreme Court was false, instead of taking it back, he resorted to another false charge to sustain the infamy of it. He also charged President Buchanan with having been a party to the conspiracy. I directed his attention to the fact that the charge could not possibly be true, for the reason, that at the time specified, Mr. Buchanan was not in America, but was three thousand miles off, representing the United States at the Court of St. James,[36] and had been there for a year previous, and did not return until three years afterward. Yet I never could get Mr. Lincoln to take back his false charge, although I have called upon him over and over again. He refuses to do it, and either remains silent, or resorts to other tricks to try and palm his slander off on the country. Therein you will find the difference between Mr. Lincoln and myself. When I make a mistake,

---

[36] That is, Great Britain.

as an honest man I correct it without being asked to do so; but when he makes a false charge, he sticks to it, and never corrects it. One word more in regard to these resolutions: I quoted them at Ottawa merely to ask Mr. Lincoln whether he stood on that platform. That was the purpose for which I quoted them. I did not think that I had a right to put idle questions to him, and I first laid a foundation for my questions by showing that the principles which I wished him either to affirm or deny had been adopted by some portion of his friends, at least, as their creed. Hence, I read the resolutions and put the questions to him; and he then refused to answer them. Subsequently, one week afterward, he did answer a part of them, but the others he has not answered up to this day. . . .

The Dred Scott decision was pronounced by the highest tribunal on earth. From that decision there is no appeal this side of Heaven. Yet, Mr. Lincoln says he is going to reverse that decision. By what tribunal will he reverse it? Will he appeal to a mob? Does he intend to appeal to violence, to lynch law? Will he stir up strife and rebellion in the land, and overthrow the court by violence? He does not deign to tell you how he will reverse the Dred Scott decision, but keeps appealing each day from the Supreme Court of the United States to political meetings in the country. He wants me to argue with you the merits of each point of that decision before this political meeting. I say to you, with all due respect, that I choose to abide by the decisions of the Supreme Court as they are pronounced. It is not for me to inquire, after a decision is made, whether I like it in all the points or not. When I used to practice law with Lincoln, I never knew him to be beat in a case that he did not get mad at the judge, and talk about appealing; and when I got beat, I generally thought the court was wrong, but I never dreamed of going out of the court house and making a stump speech to the people against the judge, merely because I had found out that I did not know the law as well as he did. If the decision did not suit me, I appealed until I got to the Supreme Court; and then if that court, the highest tribunal in the world, decided against me, I was satisfied, because it is the duty of every law-abiding man to obey the constitutions, the laws, and the constituted authorities. He who attempts to stir up odium and rebellion in the country against the constituted authorities, is stimulating the passions of men to resort to violence and to mobs instead of to the law. Hence, I tell you that I take the decisions of the Supreme Court as the law of the land, and I intend to obey them as such.

But Mr. Lincoln says that I will not answer his question as to what I would do in the event of the court making so ridiculous a decision as he imagines they would by deciding that the free State of Illinois could not prohibit slavery within her own limits. I told him at Freeport why I would not answer such a question. I told him that there was not a man possessing any brains in America, lawyer or not, who ever dreamed that such a thing could be done. I told him then, as I do now, that by all the principles set forth in the Dred Scott decision, it is impossible. I told him then, as I do now, that it is an insult to men's understanding, and a gross calumny on the court, to presume in advance that it was going to degrade itself so low as to make a decision known to be in direct violation of the Constitution. . . .

If each State will only agree to mind its own business and let its neighbors alone, there will be peace forever between us. We in Illinois tried slavery when a Territory, and found it was not good for us in this climate, and with our surroundings, and hence we abolished it. We then adopted a Free State Constitution, as we had a right to do. In this State we have declared that a negro shall not be a citizen, and we have also declared that he shall not be a slave. We had a right to adopt that policy. Missouri has just as good a right to adopt the other policy. I am now speaking of rights under the Constitution, and not of moral or religious rights. I do not discuss the morals of the people of Missouri, but let them settle that matter for themselves. I hold that the people of the slaveholding States are civilized men as well as ourselves, and that they bear consciences as well as we, and that they are accountable to God and their posterity, and not to us. It is for them to decide, therefore, the moral and religious right of the slavery question for themselves, within their own limits. I assert that they had as much right under the Constitution to adopt the system of policy which they have as we had to adopt ours. So it is with every other State in this Union. Let each State stand firmly by that great constitutional right, let each State mind its own business and let its neighbors alone, and there will be no trouble on this question. If we will stand by that principle, then Mr. Lincoln will find that this Republic can exist forever, divided into Free and Slave States, as our fathers made it and the people of each State have decided. Stand by that great principle, and we can go on as we have done, increasing in wealth, in population, in power, and in all the elements of greatness, until we shall be the admiration and terror of the world. We can go on and enlarge as our population increases, require more room, until we make this continent one ocean-bound republic. Under that principle the United States can perform that great mission, that destiny, which Providence has marked out for us. Under that principle we can receive with entire safety that stream of intelligence which is constantly flowing from the Old World to the New, filling up our prairies, clearing our wildernesses and building cities, towns, railroads, and other internal improvements, and thus make this the asylum of the oppressed of the whole earth. We have this great mission to perform, and it can only be performed by adhering faithfully to that principle of self-government on which our institutions were all established. I repeat that the principle is the right of each State, each Territory, to decide this slavery question for itself, to have slavery or not, as it chooses; and it does not become Mr. Lincoln, or anybody else, to tell the people of Kentucky that they have no consciences, that they are living in a state of iniquity, and that they are cherishing an institution to their bosoms in violation of the law of God. Better for him to adopt the doctrine of "judge not, lest ye shall be judged." Let him perform his own duty at home, and he will have a better fate in the future. I think there are objects of charity enough in the Free States to excite the sympathies and open the pockets of all the benevolence we have amongst us, without going abroad in search of negroes, of whose condition we know nothing. We have enough objects of charity at home, and it is our duty to take care of our own poor and our own suffering, before we go abroad to intermeddle with other people's business.

My friends, I am told that my time is within two minutes of expiring. I have omitted many topics that I would like to have discussed before you at length. There were many points touched by Mr. Lincoln that I have not been able to take up for the want of time. I have hurried over each subject that I have discussed as rapidly as possible, so as to omit but few, but one hour and a half is not time sufficient for a man to discuss at length one half of the great questions which are now dividing the public mind.

In conclusion, I desire to return to you my grateful acknowledgements for the kindness and the courtesy with which you have listened to me. It is something remarkable that in an audience as vast as this, composed of men of opposite politics and views, with their passions highly excited, there should be so much courtesy, kindness, and respect exhibited not only toward one another, but toward the speakers; and I feel that it is due to you that I should thus express my gratitude for the kindness with which you have treated me.

MR. LINCOLN'S REJOINDER

My Friends: Since Judge Douglas has said to you in his conclusion that he had not time in an hour and a half to answer all I had said in an hour, it follows of course that I will not be able to answer in half an hour all that he said in an hour and a half.

I wish to return to Judge Douglas my profound thanks for his public annunciation here to-day, to be put on record, that his system of policy in regard to the institution of slavery contemplates that it shall last forever. We are getting a little nearer the true issue of this controversy, and I am profoundly grateful for this one sentence. Judge Douglas asks you, "Why cannot the institution of slavery, or rather, why cannot the nation, part slave and part free, continue as our fathers made it, forever?" In the first place, I insist that our fathers did not make this nation half slave and half free, or part slave and part free. I insist that they found the institution of slavery existing here. They did not make it so, but they left it so because they knew no way to get rid of it at that time. When Judge Douglas undertakes to say that, as a matter of choice, the fathers of the Government made this nation part slave and part free, he assumes what is historically a falsehood. More than that, when the fathers of the Government cut off the source of slavery by the abolition of the slave trade, and adopted a system of restricting it from the new Territories where it had not existed, I maintain that they placed it where they understood, and all sensible men understood, it was in the course of ultimate extinction; and when Judge Douglas asks me why it cannot continue as our fathers made it, I ask him why he and his friends could not let it remain as our fathers made it?

It is precisely all I ask of him in relation to the institution of slavery, that it shall be placed upon the basis that our fathers placed it upon. Mr. Brooks,[37] of South Carolina, once said, and truly said, that when this Government was established, no one expected the institution of slavery to last until this day, and that the men who formed this Government were wiser and better than the men of these days; but the men of these days had experience which the fathers had not, and that experience had taught them the invention of the cotton-gin,[38] and this had made the perpetuation of the institution of slavery a necessity in this country. Judge Douglas could not let it stand upon the basis upon which our fathers placed it, but removed it, and put it upon the cotton-gin basis. It is a question, therefore, for him and his friends to answer, why they could not let it remain where the fathers of the Government originally placed it. . . .

---

[37] United States Senator P. W. Brooks of South Carolina.

[38] The invention of the cotton-gin by Eli Whitney in 1795 made slavery more profitable and placed the opposition on an economic rather than an ethical basis.

The truth about the matter is this: Judge Douglas has sung paeans to his "Popular Sovereignty" doctrine until his Supreme Court, cooperating with him, has squatted his Squatter Sovereignty out.[39] But he will keep up this species of humbuggery about Squatter Sovereignty. He has at last invented this sort of do-nothing Sovereignty,—that the people may exclude slavery by a sort of "Sovereignty" that is exercised by doing nothing at all. Is not that running his Popular Sovereignty down awfully? Has it not got down as thin as the homeopathic soup that was made by boiling the shadow of a pigeon that had starved to death? But at last, when it is brought to the test of close reasoning, there is not even that thin decoction of it left. It is a presumption impossible in the domain of thought. It is precisely no other than the putting of that most unphilosophical proposition, that two bodies can occupy the same space at the same time. The Dred Scott decision covers the whole ground, and while it occupies it, there is no room even for the shadow of a starved pigeon to occupy the same ground. . . .

The Judge wants to know why I won't withdraw the charge in regard to a conspiracy to make slavery national, as he has withdrawn the one he made. May it please his worship, I will withdraw it when it is proven false on me as that was proven false on him. I will add a little more than that. I will withdraw it whenever a reasonable man shall be brought to believe that the charge is not true. I have asked Judge Douglas's attention to certain matters of fact tending to prove the charge of a conspiracy to nationalize slavery, and he says he convinces me that this is all untrue because Buchanan was not in the country at that time, and because the Dred Scott case had not then got into the Supreme Court; and he says that I say the Democratic owners of Dred Scott got up the case. I never did say that. I defy Judge Douglas to show that I ever said so, for I never uttered it.

[One of Mr. Douglas's reporters gesticulated affirmatively at Mr. Lincoln.]

---

[39] That is, the Dred Scott decision killed the theory of Squatter Sovereignty.

I don't care if your hireling does say I did, I tell you myself that I never said the "Democratic" owners of Dred Scott got up the case. I have never pretended to know whether Dred Scott's owners were Democrats, or Abolitionists, or Free Soilers, or Border Ruffians.[40] I have said that there is evidence about the case tending to show that it was a made-up case, for the purpose of getting that decision. I have said that that evidence was very strong in the fact that when Dred Scott was declared to be a slave, the owner of him made him free, showing that he had had the case tried and the question settled for such use as could be made of that decision; he cared nothing about the property thus declared to be his by that decision. But my time is out, and I can say no more.

---

[40] People who believed that the Territories should be admitted as free states were known as Free Soilers. During the disturbances in Kansas Territory, some emigrants came over from Missouri favoring slavery, and to them the free soil residents gave the name of Border Ruffians.

SEVENTH JOINT DEBATE

Alton, October 15, 1858

SENATOR DOUGLAS'S SPEECH

Ladies and Gentlemen: It is now nearly four months since the canvass between Mr. Lincoln and myself commenced. . . .

I hold that there is no power on earth, under our system of Government, which has the right to force a Constitution upon an unwilling people. . . .

Most of the men who denounced my course on the Lecompton question objected to it, not because I was not right, but because they thought it expedient at that time, for the sake of keeping the party together, to do wrong. . . .

But I am told that I would have been all right if I had voted for the English bill[41] after the Lecompton measure was killed. You know a pardon was granted to all political offenders on the Lecompton question, provided they would only vote for the English bill. I did not accept the benefits of that pardon, for the reason that I had been right in the course I had pursued, and hence did not require any forgiveness. Let us see how the result has been worked out. English brought in his bill referring the Lecompton Constitution back to the people, with the provision that if it was rejected, Kansas should be kept out of the Union until she had the full ratio of population required for a

---

[41] The English bill for the admission of Kansas, introduced in Congress by Wm. H. English of Indiana, is explained by Douglas in the lines which follow.

member of Congress,—thus in effect declaring that if the people of Kansas would only consent to come into the Union under the Lecompton Constitution, and have a Slave State when they did not want it, they should be admitted with a population of 35,000; but that if they were so obstinate as to insist upon having just such a constitution as they thought best, and to desire admission as a Free State, then they should be kept out until they had 93,420 inhabitants. I then said, and I now repeat to you, that whenever Kansas has people enough for a Slave State she has people enough for a Free State. I was and am willing to adopt the rule that no State shall ever come into the Union until she has the full ratio of population for a member of Congress, provided that rule is made uniform. . . .

Fellow-citizens, how have the supporters of the English bill stood up to their pledges not to admit Kansas until she obtained a population of 93,420 in the event she rejected the Lecompton Constitution? How? The newspapers inform us that English himself, whilst conducting his canvass for re-election, and in order to secure it, pledged himself to his constituents that if returned he would disregard his own bill, and vote to admit Kansas into the Union with such population as she might have when she made application. We are informed that every Democratic candidate for Congress in all the States where elections have recently been held was pledged against the English bill, with perhaps one or two exceptions. Now, if I had only done as these anti-Lecompton men who voted for the English bill in Congress, pledging themselves to refuse to admit Kansas if she refused to become a Slave State until she had a population of 93,420, and then returned to their people, forfeited their pledge, and made a new pledge to admit Kansas at any time she applied, without regard to population, I would have had no trouble. You saw the whole power and patronage of the Federal Government wielded in Indiana, Ohio, and Pennsylvania to re-elect anti-Lecompton men to Congress who voted against Lecompton, then voted for the English bill, and then denounced the English bill, and pledged themselves to their people to disregard it. My sin consists in not having given a pledge, and then in not having afterward forfeited it. For that reason, in this State, every postmaster, every route agent, every collector of the ports, and every Federal office-holder, forfeits his head the moment he expresses a preference for the Democratic candidates against Lincoln and his Abolition associates. A Democratic Administration[42] which we helped to bring into power, deems it consistent with its fidelity to principle and its regard to duty to wield its power in this State on behalf of the Republican Abolition candidates, in every county and every Congressional District against the Democratic party. All I have to say in reference to the matter is, that if that Administration have not regard enough for principle, if they are not sufficiently attached to the creed of the Democratic party, to bury forever their personal hostilities in order to succeed in carrying out our glorious principles, I have. I have no personal difficulty with Mr. Buchanan or his Cabinet. He chose to make certain recommendations to Congress, as he had a right to do, on the Lecompton question. I could not vote in favor of them. I had as much right to judge for myself how I should vote as he had how he should recommend. He undertook to say to me, "If you do not vote as I tell you, I will take off the heads of your friends." I replied to him, "You did not elect me; I represent Illinois, and I am accountable to Illinois, as my constituency, and to God; but not to the President or to any other power on earth."

And now this warfare is made on me because I would not surrender my convictions of duty, because I would not abandon my constituency, and receive the orders of the executive authorities how I should vote in the Senate of the United States. I hold that an attempt to control the Senate on the part of the Executive is subversive of the principles of our Constitution. The Executive department is independent of the

---

[42] Douglas, a Democrat, had incurred the displeasure of Buchanan, a Democratic president, on the Kansas question, because the senator refused to support the Lecompton constitution.

Senate, and the Senate is independent of the President. In matters of legislation the President has a veto on the action of the Senate, and in appointments and treaties the Senate has a veto on the President. He has no more right to tell me how I shall vote on his appointments than I have to tell him whether he shall veto or approve a bill that the Senate has passed. Whenever you recognize the right of the Executive to say to a Senator, "Do this, or I will take off the heads of your friends," you convert this Government from a republic into a despotism. Whenever you recognize the right of a President to say to a member of Congress, "Vote as I tell you, or I will bring a power to bear against you at home which will crush you," you destroy the independence of the Representative, and convert him into a tool of Executive power. I resisted this invasion of the constitutional rights of a Senator, and I intend to resist it as long as I have a voice to speak or a vote to give. Yet, Mr. Buchanan cannot provoke me to abandon one iota of Democratic principles out of revenge or hostility to his course. I stand by the platform of the Democratic party, and by its organization, and support its nominees. If there are any who choose to bolt, the fact only shows that they are not as good Democrats as I am. . . .

I hold that this Government was established on the white basis. It was established by white men for the benefit of white men and their posterity forever, and should be administered by white men, and none others. But it does not follow, by any means, that merely because the negro is not a citizen, and merely because he is not our equal, that, therefore, he should be a slave. On the contrary, it does follow that we ought to extend to the negro race, and to all other dependent races, all the rights, all the privileges, and all the immunities which they can exercise consistently with the safety of society. Humanity requires that we should give them all these privileges; Christianity commands that we should extend those privileges to them. The question then arises, what are those privileges, and what is the nature and extent of them. My answer is that that is a question which each State must answer for itself. . . . If the people of all the States will act on that great principle, and each State mind its own business, attend to its own affairs, take care of its own negroes, and not meddle with its neighbors, then there will be peace between the North and South, the East and the West, throughout the whole Union.

Why can we not thus have peace? Why should we thus allow a sectional party to agitate this country, to array the North against the South, and convert us into enemies instead of friends, merely that a few ambitious men may ride into power on a sectional hobby? How long is it since these ambitious Northern men wished for a sectional organization? Did any one of them dream of a sectional party as long as the North was the weaker section and the South the stronger? Then all were opposed to sectional parties; but the moment the North obtained the majority in the House and Senate by the admission of California, and could elect a President without the aid of Southern votes, that moment ambitious Northern men formed a scheme to excite the North against the South, and make the people be governed in their votes by geographical lines, thinking that the North, being the stronger section, would outvote the South, and consequently they, the leaders, would ride into office on a sectional hobby. I am told that my hour is out. It was very short.

MR. LINCOLN'S REPLY

Ladies and Gentlemen: I have been somewhat, in my own mind, complimented by a large portion of Judge Douglas's speech,—I mean that portion which he devotes to the controversy between himself and the present Administration. This is the seventh time Judge Douglas and myself have met in these joint discussions, and he has been gradually improving in regard to his war with the Administration. At Quincy, day before yesterday, he was a little more severe upon the Administration than I had heard him upon any occasion, and I took pains to compliment him for it. I then told him to "Give it to them with all the power he had," and as some of

them were present, I told them I would be very much obliged
if they would give it to him in about the same way. I take it
he has now vastly improved upon the attack he made then
upon the Administration. I flatter myself he has really taken
my advice on this subject. All I can say now is to recommend
to him and to them what I then commended,—to prosecute
the war against one another in the most vigorous manner. I say
to them again: "Go it, husband!—Go it, bear!"[43]. . . .

You have heard him frequently allude to my controversy
with him in regard to the Declaration of Independence. . . .

At Galesburg, the other day, I said in answer to Judge
Douglas, that three years ago there never had been a man, so
far as I knew or believed, in the whole world, who had said
that the Declaration of Independence did not include negroes
in the term "all men." I reassert it to-day. I assert that Judge
Douglas and all his friends may search the whole records of
the country, and it will be a matter of great astonishment to
me if they shall be able to find that one human being three
years ago had ever uttered the astounding sentiment, that the
term "all men" in the Declaration did not include the negro.
Do not let me be misunderstood. I know that more than three
years ago there were men who, finding this assertion constantly in the way of their schemes to bring about the ascen-
dency and perpetuation of slavery, denied the truth of it. I
know that Mr. Calhoun and all the politicians of his school
denied the truth of the Declaration. I know that it ran along
in the mouth of some Southern men for a period of years,
ending at last in that shameful, though rather forcible declaration of Pettit[44] of Indiana, upon the floor of the United States
Senate, that the Declaration of Independence was in that
respect "a self-evident lie," rather than a self-evident truth.

---

[43] A local story current at the time about a woman who saw her worthless
husband attacked by a bear. She refused to help either man or bear, trust-
ing that each would kill the other.

[44] Hon. John Pettit of Indiana was U. S. Senator, 1853–5, and later was
appointed by President Buchanan chief justice of Kansas Territory.

But I say, with a perfect knowledge of all this hawking at the Declaration without directly attacking it, that three years ago there never had lived a man who had ventured to assail it in the sneaking way of pretending to believe it, and then asserting it did not include the negro. I believe the first man who ever said it was Chief Justice Taney in the Dred Scott case, and the next to him was our friend Stephen A. Douglas. And now it has become the catchword of the entire party. . . .

And when this new principle—this new proposition that no human being ever thought of three years ago—is brought forward, I combat it as having an evil tendency, if not an evil design. I combat it as having a tendency to dehumanize the negro, to take away from him the right of ever striving to be a man. I combat it as being one of the thousand things constantly done in these days to prepare the public mind to make property, and nothing but property, of the negro in all the States of this Union. . . .

Judge Douglas has again referred to a Springfield speech in which I said "a house divided against itself cannot stand." The Judge has so often made the entire quotation from that speech that I can make it from memory. I used this language:—

We are now far into the fifth year since a policy was initiated with the avowed object and confident promise of putting an end to the slavery agitation. Under the operation of this policy, that agitation has not only not ceased, but has constantly augmented. In my opinion it will not cease until a crisis shall have been reached and passed. "A house divided against itself cannot stand." I believe this Government cannot endure permanently, half slave and half free. I do not expect the house to fall, but I do expect it will cease to be divided. It will become all one thing, or all the other. Either the opponents of slavery will arrest the further spread of it, and place it where the public mind shall rest in the belief that it is in the course of ultimate extinction, or its advocates will push it forward till it shall become alike lawful in all the States,—old as well as new, North as well as South.

That extract and the sentiments expressed in it have been extremely offensive to Judge Douglas. He has warred upon them as Satan wars upon the Bible. His perversions upon it are endless. Here now are my views upon it in brief.

I said we were now far into the fifth year since a policy was initiated with the avowed object and confident promise of putting an end to the slavery agitation. Is it not so? When that Nebraska bill was brought forward four years ago last January, was it not for the "avowed object" of putting an end to the slavery agitation? We were to have no more agitation in Congress; it was all to be banished to the Territories. By the way, I will remark here that, as Judge Douglas is very fond of complimenting Mr. Crittenden[45] in these days, Mr. Crittenden has said there was a falsehood in that whole business, for there was no slavery agitation at that time to allay. We were for a little while quiet on the troublesome thing, and that very allaying plaster of Judge Douglas's stirred it up again. But was it not understood or intimated, with the "confident promise" of putting an end to the slavery agitation? Surely it was. In every speech you heard Judge Douglas make, until he got into this "imbroglio," as they call it, with the Administration about the Lecompton Constitution, every speech on that Nebraska bill was full of his felicitation that we were just at the end of the slavery agitation. The last tip of the last joint of the old serpent's tail was just drawing out of view. But has it proved so? I have asserted that under that policy that agitation "has not only not ceased, but has constantly augmented." When was there ever a greater agitation in Congress than last winter? When was it as great in the country as to-day.

There was a collateral object in the introduction of that Nebraska policy, which was to clothe the people of the Territories with a superior degree of self-government, beyond what they had ever had before. The first object and the main one of conferring upon the people a higher degree of "self-government" is a question of fact, to be determined by you in answer to a single question. Have you ever heard or known of a people anywhere on earth who had as little to do as, in

---

[45] Senator John J. Crittenden of Kentucky.

the first instance of its use, the people of Kansas had with this same right of "self-government?" In its main policy and in its collateral object, it has been nothing but a living, creeping lie from the time of its introduction till to-day.

I have intimated that I thought the agitation would not cease until a crisis should have been reached and passed. I have stated in what way I thought it would be reached and passed. I have said that it might go one way or the other. We might, by arresting the further spread of it, and placing it where the fathers originally placed it, put it where the public mind should rest in the belief that it was in the course of ultimate extinction. Thus the agitation may cease. It may be pushed forward until it shall become alike lawful in all the States, old as well as new, North as well as South. I have said, and I repeat, my wish is that the further spread of it may be arrested, and that it may be placed where the public mind shall rest in the belief that it is in the course of ultimate extinction. I have expressed that as my wish. I entertain the opinion, upon evidence sufficient to my mind, that the fathers of this Government placed that institution where the public mind did rest in the belief that it was in the course of ultimate extinction. Let me ask why they made provision that the source of slavery—the African slave trade— should be cut off at the end of twenty years? Why did they make provision that in all the new territory we owned at that time slavery should be forever inhibited? Why stop its spread in one direction, and cut off its source in another, if they did not look to its being placed in the course of ultimate extinction?

Again: the institution of slavery is only mentioned in the Constitution of the United States two or three times, and in neither of these cases does the word "slavery" or "negro race" occur; but covert language is used each time, and for a purpose full of significance. What is the language in regard to the prohibition of the African slave-trade? It runs in about this way:—

The migration or importation of such persons as any of the States now existing shall think proper to admit, shall not be prohibited by the Congress prior to the year one thousand eight hundred and eight.

The next allusion in the Constitution to the question of slavery and the black race, is on the subject of the basis of representation, and there the language used is:—

Representatives and direct taxes shall be apportioned among the several States which may be included within this Union, according to their respective numbers, which shall be determined by adding to the whole number of free persons, including those bound to service for a term of years, and excluding Indians not taxed,—three-fifths of all other persons.

It says "persons," not slaves, not negroes; but this "three-fifths" can be applied to no other class among us than the negroes.

Lastly, in the provision for the reclamation of fugitive slaves, it is said:—

No person held to service or labor in one State, under the laws thereof, escaping into another, shall, in consequence of any law or regulation therein, be discharged from such service or labor, but shall be delivered up, on claim of the party to whom such service or labor may be due.

There again there is no mention of the word "negro," or of slavery. In all three of these places, being the only allusions to slavery in the instrument, covert language is used. Language is used not suggesting that slavery existed or that the black race were among us. And I understand the contemporaneous history of those times to be that covert language was used with a purpose, and that purpose was that in our Constitution, which it was hoped and is still hoped will endure forever,—when it should be read by intelligent and patriotic men, after the institution of slavery had passed from among us,—there should be nothing on the face of the great charter of liberty suggesting that such a thing as negro slavery had ever existed among us. This is part of the evidence that the fathers of the Government expected and intended the institution of slavery to come to an end. They expected and intended that it should be in the course of ultimate extinction. And when I say that I desire to see the further spread of it arrested, I only say I desire to see that done which the fathers have first done. When I say I desire to see it placed where the public mind will rest in the belief that it is in the course of ultimate extinction, I only say I desire to see it placed where they placed it. It is not true that our fathers, as Judge Douglas assumes, made this Government part slave and part free. Understand the sense in which he puts it. He assumes that slavery is a rightful thing within itself,—was introduced by the framers of the Constitution. The exact truth is, that they found the institution existing among us, and they left it as they found it. But in making the Government they left this institution with many clear marks of disapprobation upon it. They found slavery among them, and they left it among them because of the difficulty—the absolute impossibility—of its immediate removal. And when Judge Douglas asks me why we cannot let it remain part slave and part free, as the fathers of the Government made it, he asks a question based upon an assumption which is itself a falsehood; and I turn upon him and ask him the question, when the policy that the fathers of the Government had adopted in relation to this element among us was the best policy in the world, the only wise policy, the only policy that we can ever safely continue upon, that will ever give us peace, unless this dangerous element masters us all and becomes a national institution,—I turn upon him and ask him why he could not leave it alone. I turn and ask him why he was driven to the necessity of introducing a new policy in regard to it. He has himself said he introduced a new policy. He said so in his speech on the 22d of March of the present year, 1858. I ask him why he could not let it remain where our fathers placed it. I ask, too, of Judge Douglas and his friends, why we shall not again place this institution upon the basis on which the fathers left it. I ask you, when he infers that I am in favor of setting the Free and Slave States at war, when the institution was placed in that attitude by those who made the Constitution, did they make any war? If we had no war out of it when thus placed, wherein is the ground of belief that we shall have war out of it if we return to that policy? Have we had any peace upon this matter springing from any other basis?

I maintain that we have not. I have proposed nothing more than a return to the policy of the fathers.

I confess, when I propose a certain measure of policy, it is not enough for me that I do not intend anything evil in the result, but it is incumbent on me to show that it has not a tendency to that result. I have met Judge Douglas in that point of view. I have not only made the declaration that I do not mean to produce a conflict between the States, but I have tried to show by fair reasoning, and I think I have shown to the minds of fair men, that I propose nothing but what has a most peaceful tendency. The quotation that I happened to make in that Springfield speech, that "a house divided against itself cannot stand," and which has proved so offensive to the Judge, was part and parcel of the same thing. He tries to show that variety in the domestic institutions of the different States is necessary and indispensable. I do not dispute it. I have no controversy with Judge Douglas about that. I shall very readily agree with him that it would be foolish for us to insist upon having a cranberry law here in Illinois where we have no cranberries, because they have a cranberry law in Indiana, where they have cranberries. I should insist that it would be exceedingly wrong in us to deny to Virginia the right to enact oyster laws, where they have oysters, because we want no such laws here. I understand, I hope, quite as well as Judge Douglas or anybody else, that the variety in the soil and climate and face of the country, and consequent variety in the industrial pursuits and productions of a country, require systems of law conforming to this variety in the natural features of the country. I understand quite as well as Judge Douglas, that if we here raise a barrel of flour more than we want, and the Louisianians raise a barrel of sugar more than they want, it is of mutual advantage to exchange. That produces commerce, brings us together, and makes us better friends. We like one another the more for it. And I understand as well as Judge Douglas, or anybody else, that these mutual accommodations are the cements which bind together the different parts of this Union; that instead of being a thing to "divide the house,"—figuratively expressing the Union,—they tend to sustain it; they are the props of the house, tending always to hold it up.

But when I have admitted all this, I ask if there is any parallel between these things and this institution of slavery. I do not see that there is any parallel at all between them. Consider it. When have we had any difficulty or quarrel amongst ourselves about the cranberry laws of Indiana, or the oyster laws of Virginia, or the pine-lumber laws of Maine, or the fact that Louisiana produces sugar, and Illinois flour? When have we had any quarrels over these things? When have we had perfect peace in regard to this thing which I say is an element of discord in this Union. We have sometimes had peace, but when was it? It was when the institution of slavery remained quiet where it was. We have had difficulty and turmoil whenever it has made a struggle to spread itself where it was not. I ask, then, if experience does not speak in thunder-tones, telling us that the policy which has given peace to the country heretofore, being returned to, gives the greatest promise of peace again. You may say, and Judge Douglas has intimated the same thing, that all this difficulty in regard to the institution of slavery is the mere agitation of office-seekers and ambitious northern politicians. He thinks we want to get "his place," I suppose. I agree that there are office-seekers amongst us. The Bible says somewhere that we are desperately selfish. I think we would have discovered that fact without the Bible. I do not claim that I am any less so than the average of men, but I do claim that I am not more selfish than Judge Douglas.

But is it true that all the difficulty and agitation we have in regard to this institution of slavery springs from office-seeking, from the mere ambition of politicians? Is that the truth? How many times have we had danger from this question? Go back to the day of the Missouri Compromise. Go back to the Nullification question, at the bottom of which lay this same slavery question. Go back to the time of the annexation of Texas. Go back to the troubles that led to the Compromise of 1850. You will find that every time, with the single exception of the Nullification question, they sprung from an endeavor to spread this institution. There never was a party in the history of this country, and there probably never will be, of sufficient strength to disturb the general peace of the country. Parties themselves may be divided and quarrel on minor questions, yet it extends not beyond the parties themselves. But does not this question make a disturbance outside of political circles? Does it not enter into the churches and rend them asunder? What divided the great Methodist church into two parts, North and South? What has raised this constant disturbance in every Presbyterian General Assembly that meets? What disturbed the Unitarian Church in this very city two years ago? What has jarred and shaken the great American Tract Society recently, not yet splitting it, but sure to divide it in the end? Is it not this same mighty, deep-seated power that somehow operates on the minds of men, exciting and stirring them up in every avenue of society,—in politics, in religion, in literature, in morals, in all the manifold relations of life? Is this the work of politicians? Is that irresistible power, which for fifty years has shaken the Government and agitated the people, to be stilled and subdued by pretending that it is an exceedingly simple thing, and we ought not to talk about it? If you will get everybody else to stop talking about it, I assure you I will quit before they have half done so. But where is the philosophy or statesmanship which assumes that you can quiet that disturbing element in our society which has disturbed us for more than half a century, which has been the only serious danger that has threatened our institutions,—I say, where is the philosophy or the statesmanship based on the assumption that we are to quit talking about it, and that the public mind is all at once to cease being agitated by it! Yet this is the policy here in the North that Douglas is advocating,—that we are to care nothing about it! I ask you if it is not a false philosophy? Is it not a false statesmanship that undertakes to build up a system of policy upon the basis of caring nothing about the very thing that everybody does care the most about?—a thing which all experience has shown we care a very great deal about?

The Judge alludes very often in the course of his remarks to the exclusive right which the States have to decide the whole thing for themselves. I agree with him very readily that the different States have that right. . . . What I insist upon is, that the new Territories shall be kept free from it while in the Territorial condition. Judge Douglas assumes that we have no interest in them,—that we have no right whatever to interfere. I think we have some interest. I think that as white men we have. Do we not wish for an outlet for our surplus population, if I may so express myself? Do we not feel an interest in getting to that outlet with such institutions as we would like to have prevail there? If you go to a Territory opposed to slavery, and another man comes upon the same ground with his slave, upon the assumption that the things are equal, it turns out that he has the equal right all his way, and you have no part of it your way. If he goes in and makes it a Slave Territory, and, by consequence, a Slave State, is it not time that those who desire to have it a Free State were on equal ground? Let me suggest it in a different way. How many Democrats are there about here ["A thousand."] who have left Slave States and come into the Free State of Illinois to get rid of the institution of slavery? [Another voice: "A thousand and one."] I reckon there are a thousand and one. I will ask you, if the policy you are now advocating had prevailed when this country was in a Territorial condition, where would you have gone to get rid of it? Where would you have found your Free State or Territory to go to? And when hereafter, for any cause, the people in this place shall desire to find new homes, if they wish to be rid of the institution, where will they find the place to go to?

Now, irrespective of the moral aspect of this question as to whether there is a right or wrong in enslaving a negro, I am still in favor of our new Territories being in such a condition that white men may find a home,—may find some spot where they can better their condition; where they can settle upon new soil and better their condition in life. I am in favor of this, not merely (I must say it here as I have elsewhere) for our own people who are born amongst us, but as an outlet for free white people everywhere, the world over,—in which Hans, and Baptiste, and Patrick, and all other men from all the world, may find new homes and better their conditions in life.

I understand I have ten minutes yet. I will employ it in saying something about this argument Judge Douglas uses, while he sustains the Dred Scott decision, that the people of the Territories can still somehow exclude slavery. The first thing I ask attention to is the fact that Judge Douglas constantly said, before the decision, that whether they could or not was a question for the Supreme Court. But after the court has made the decision he virtually says it is not a question for the Supreme Court, but for the people. And how is it he tells us they can exclude it? He says it needs "police regulations," and that it admits of "unfriendly legislation." Although it is a right established by the Constitution of the United States to take a slave into a Territory of the United States and hold him as property, yet unless the Territorial Legislature will give friendly legislation, and, more especially, if they adopt unfriendly legislation, they can practically exclude him. Now, without meeting this proposition as a matter of fact, I pass to consider the real constitutional obligation. Let me take the gentleman who looks me in the face before me, and let us suppose that he is a member of the Territorial Legislature. The first thing he will do will be to swear that he will support the Constitution of the United States. His neighbor by his side in the Territory has slaves and needs Territorial legislation to enable him to enjoy that constitutional right. Can he withhold the legislation which his neighbor needs for the enjoyment of a right which is fixed in his favor in the Constitution of the United States which he has sworn to support? Can he withhold it without violating his oath? And, more especially, can he pass unfriendly legislation to violate his oath? Why, this is a monstrous sort of talk about the Constitution of the United States! There has never been as outlandish or lawless a doctrine from the mouth of any respectable man on earth. I do not believe it is a constitutional right to hold slaves in a Territory of the United States. I believe the decision was improperly made. I go for reversing it. Judge Douglas is furious against those who go for reversing a decision. But he is for legislating it out of all force while the law itself stands. I repeat that there has never been so monstrous a doctrine uttered from the mouth of a respectable man.

I suppose most of us (I know it of myself) believe that the people of the Southern States are entitled to a Congressional Fugitive Slave law,—that is a right fixed in the Constitution. But it cannot be made available to them without Congressional legislation. In the Judge's language, it is a "barren right," which needs legislation before it can become efficient and valuable to the persons to whom it is guaranteed. And as the right is constitutional, I agree that the legislation shall be granted to it,—and that not that we like the institution of slavery. We profess we have no taste for running and catching niggers,—at least, I profess no taste for that job at all. Why then do I yield support to a Fugitive Slave law? Because I do not understand that the Constitution, which guarantees that right, can be supported without it. And if I believed that the right to hold a slave in a Territory was equally fixed in the Constitution with the right to reclaim fugitives, I should be bound to give it the legislation necessary to support it. I say that no man can deny his obligation to give the necessary legislation to support slavery in a Territory, who believes it is a constitutional right to have it there. No man can, who does not give the Abolitionists an argument to deny the obligation enjoined by the Constitution to enact a Fugitive Slave law. Try it now. It is the strongest Abolition argument ever made. I say, if that Dred Scott decision is correct, then the right to hold slaves in a Territory is equally a constitutional right with the right of a slaveholder to have his runaway returned. No one can show the distinction between them. The one is express, so that we cannot deny it. The other is construed to be in the Constitution, so that he who believed the decision to be correct believes in the right. And the man who argues that by unfriendly legislation, in spite of that constitutional right, slavery may be driven from the Territories, cannot avoid furnishing an argument by which Abolitionists may deny the obligation to return fugitives, and claim the power to pass laws unfriendly to the right of the slaveholder to reclaim his fugitive. I do not know how such an argument may strike a popular assembly like this, but I defy anybody to go before a body of men whose minds are educated to estimating evidence and reasoning, and show that there is an iota of difference between the constitutional right to reclaim a fugitive, and the constitutional right to hold a slave, in a Territory, provided this Dred Scott decision is correct. I defy any man to make an argument that will justify unfriendly legislation to deprive a slaveholder of his right to hold his slave in a Territory, that will not equally, in all its length, breadth, and thickness, furnish an argument for nullifying the Fugitive Slave law. Why, there is not such an Abolitionist in the nation as Douglas, after all.

MR. DOUGLAS'S REPLY

Mr. Lincoln has concluded his remarks by saying that there is not such an Abolitionist as I am in all America. If he could make the Abolitionists of Illinois believe that, he would not have much show for the Senate. Let him make the Abolitionists believe the truth of that statement, and his political back is broken.

His first criticism upon me is the expression of his hope that the war of the Administration will be prosecuted against me and the Democratic party of this State with vigor. He wants that war prosecuted with vigor; I have no doubt of it. His hopes of success and the hopes of his party depend solely upon it. They have no chance of destroying the Democracy of this State except by the aid of Federal patronage. He has all the Federal officeholders here as his allies, running separate tickets against the Democracy to divide the party, although the leaders all intend to vote directly the Abolition ticket, and only leave the greenhorns to vote this separate ticket who refuse to go into the Abolition camp. There is something really refreshing in the thought that Mr. Lincoln is in favor of prosecuting one war vigorously. It is the first war I ever knew him to be in favor of prosecuting. It is the first war I ever knew him to believe to be just or constitutional. When the Mexican War was being waged, and the American army was surrounded by the enemy in Mexico, he thought that war was unconstitutional, unnecessary, and unjust. He thought it was not commenced on the right spot.

When I made an incidental allusion of that kind in the joint discussion over at Charleston some weeks ago, Lincoln, in replying, said that I, Douglas, had charged him with voting against supplies for the Mexican War, and then reared up, full length, and swore that he never voted against the supplies; that it was a slander, and caught hold of Ficklin,[46] who sat on the stand, and said, "Here, Ficklin, tell the people that it is a lie." Well, Ficklin, who had served in Congress with him, stood up and told them all that he recollected about it. It was that, when George Ashmun[47] of Massachusetts brought forward a resolution declaring the war unconstitutional, unnecessary, and unjust, that Lincoln had voted for it. "Yes," said Lincoln, "I did." Thus he confessed that he voted that the war was wrong, that our country was in the wrong, and consequently that the Mexicans were in the right; but charged that I had slandered him by saying that he voted against the supplies. I never charged him with voting against the supplies in my life, because I knew that he was not in Congress when they were voted. The war was commenced on the 13th day of May, 1846, and on that day we appropriated in Congress ten millions of dollars and fifty thousand men to prosecute it. During the same session we voted more men and more money, and at the next session we voted more men and more money, so that by the time Mr. Lincoln entered Congress we had enough men and enough money to carry on the war, and had no occasion to vote for any more. When he got into

---

[46] Orlando B. Ficklin of Coles County, Illinois, served with Lincoln in the state Legislature and in Congress.

[47] George Ashmun, a member of Congress from Massachusetts.

the House, being opposed to the war, and not being able to stop the supplies, because they had all gone forward, all he could do was to follow the lead of Corwin,[48] and prove that the war was not begun on the right spot, and that it was unconstitutional, unnecessary, and wrong.[49] Remember, too, that this he did after the war had been begun. It is one thing to be opposed to the declaration of a war, another and very different thing to take sides with the enemy against your own country after the war has been commenced. Our army was in Mexico at the time, many battles had been fought; our citizens, who were defending the honor of their country's flag, were surrounded by the daggers, the guns, and the poison of the enemy. Then it was that Corwin made his speech in which he declared that the American soldiers ought to be welcomed by the Mexicans with bloody hands to hospitable graves; then it was that Ashmun and Lincoln voted in the House of Representatives that the war was unconstitutional and unjust; and Ashmun's resolution, Corwin's speech, and Lincoln's vote were sent to Mexico and read at the head of the Mexican army, to prove to them that there was a Mexican party in the Congress of the United States who were doing all in their power to aid them. That a man takes sides with the common enemy against his own country in time of war should rejoice in a war being made on me now, is very natural. And, in my opinion, no other kind of a man would rejoice in it. . . .

Mr. Lincoln told you that the slavery question was the only thing that ever disturbed the peace and harmony of the Union. Did not Nullification[50] once raise its head and disturb

---

[48] Thomas Corwin of Ohio, a member of Congress, was a Whig leader who led the opposition to the Mexican War declared by a Democratic administration.

[49] The doubt of these Whig leaders concerning the justification of the war on Mexico has been gradually growing in the opinion of the American people since that day.

[50] The theory so strongly advocated by Calhoun that any state has the right

the peace of this Union in 1832? Was that the slavery question, Mr. Lincoln? Did not disunion raise its monster head during the last war with Great Britain? Was that the slavery question, Mr. Lincoln? The peace of this country has been disturbed three times, once during the war with Great Britain, once on the tariff question, and once on the slavery question. His argument, therefore, that slavery is the only question that has ever created dissension in the Union falls to the ground. It is true that agitators are enabled now to use this slavery question for the purpose of sectional strife. He admits that in regard to all things else, the principle that I advocate, making each State and Territory free to decide for itself, ought to prevail. He instances the cranberry laws and the oyster laws, and he might have gone through the whole list with the same effect. I say that all these laws are local and domestic, and that local and domestic concerns should be left to each State and each Territory to manage for itself. If agitators would acquiesce in that principle, there never would be any danger to the peace and harmony of the Union.

Mr. Lincoln tries to avoid the main issue by attacking the truth of my proposition, that our fathers made this Government divided into Free and Slave States, recognizing the right of each to decide all its local questions for itself. Did they not thus make it? It is true that they did not establish slavery in any of the States, or abolish it in any of them; but finding thirteen States, twelve of which were slave and one free, they agreed to form a Government uniting them together as they stood, divided into Free and Slave States, and to guarantee forever to each State the right to do as it pleased on the slavery question.

---

to declare null and void within its boundaries any United States law which the State thinks unconstitutional. In 1832 South Carolina declared that the tariff acts of 1828 and 1832 were null and void, and that if the Federal Government tried to enforce them in that State, the State would withdraw from the Union. President Jackson declared that he would use force to administer the law, but before this became necessary a new tariff act more favorable to the South was enacted.

Having thus made the Government, and conferred this right upon each State forever, I assert that this Government can exist as they made it, divided into Free and Slave States, if any one State chooses to retain slavery. He says that he looks forward to a time when slavery shall be abolished everywhere. I look forward to a time when each State shall be allowed to do as it pleases. If it chooses to keep slavery forever, it is not my business, but its own; if it chooses to abolish slavery, it is its own business,—not mine. I care more for the great principle of self-government, the right of the people to rule, than I do for all the negroes in Christendom. I would not endanger the perpetuity of this Union, I would not blot out the great inalienable rights of the white men, for all the negroes that ever existed. Hence, I say, let us maintain this Government on the principles that our fathers made it, recognizing the right of each State to keep slavery as long as its people determine, or to abolish it when they please. But Mr. Lincoln says that when our fathers made this Government they did not look forward to the state of things now existing, and therefore he thinks the doctrine was wrong; and he quotes Brooks, of South Carolina, to prove that our fathers then thought that probably slavery would be abolished by each State acting for itself before this time. Suppose they did; suppose they did not foresee what has occurred,—does that change the principles of our Government? They did not probably foresee the telegraph that transmits intelligence by lightning, nor did they foresee the railroads that now form the bonds of union between the different States, or the thousand mechanical inventions that have elevated mankind. But do these things change the principles of the Government? Our fathers, I say, made this Government on the principle of the right of each State to do as it pleases in its own domestic affairs, subject to the Constitution, and allowed the people of each to apply to every new change of circumstances such remedy as they may see fit to improve their condition. This right they have for all time to come.

Mr. Lincoln went on to tell you that he does not at all desire to interfere with slavery in the States where it exists, nor does his party. I expected him to say that down here. Let me ask him, then, how he expects to put slavery in the course of ultimate extinction everywhere, if he does not intend to interfere with it in the States where it exists? He says that he will prohibit it in all Territories, and the inference is, then, that unless they make Free States out of them he will keep them out of the Union; for, mark you, he did not say whether or not he would vote to admit Kansas with slavery or not, as her people might apply (he forgot that, as usual, etc.); he did not say whether or not he was in favor of bringing the Territories now in existence into the Union on the principle of Clay's Compromise measures on the slavery question. I told you that he would not. His idea is that he will prohibit slavery in all the Territories, and thus force them all to become Free States, surrounding the Slave States with a cordon of Free States, and hemming them in, keeping the slaves confined to their present limits whilst they go on multiplying, until the soil on which they live will no longer feed them, and he will thus be able to put slavery in a course of ultimate extinction by starvation. He will extinguish slavery in the Southern States as the French general exterminated the Algerines when he smoked them out. He is going to extinguish slavery by surrounding the Slave States, hemming in the slaves, and starving them out of existence, as you smoke a fox out of his hole. He intends to do that in the name of humanity and Christianity, in order that we may get rid of the terrible crime and sin entailed upon our fathers of holding slaves. Mr. Lincoln makes out that line of policy, and appeals to the moral sense of justice and to the Christian feeling of the community to sustain him. He says that any man who holds to the contrary doctrine is in the position of the king who claimed to govern by divine right. Let us examine for a moment and see what principle it was that overthrew the divine right of George the Third to govern us. Did not these Colonies rebel because the British Parliament had no right to pass laws concerning our property and domestic and private institutions without our consent! We demanded that the British Government should not pass such laws unless they gave us representation in the body passing them; and this the British Government insisting on doing, we went to war, on the principle that the Home Government should not control and govern distant colonies without giving them a representation. Now, Mr. Lincoln proposes to govern the Territories without giving them a representation, and calls on Congress to pass laws controlling their property and domestic concerns without their consent and against their will. Thus, he asserts for his party the identical principle asserted by George III and the Tories of the Revolution. . . .

My friends, if, as I have said before, we will only live up to this great fundamental principle, there will be peace between the North and the South. Mr. Lincoln admits that, under the Constitution, on all domestic questions except slavery, we ought not to interfere with the people of each State. What right have we to interfere with slavery any more than we have to interfere with any other question? He says that this slavery question is now the bone of contention. Why? Simply because agitators have combined in all the Free States to make war upon it. Suppose the agitators in the States should combine in one-half of the Union to make war upon the railroad system of the other half? They would thus be driven to the same sectional strife. Suppose one section makes war upon any other peculiar institution of the opposite section, and the same strife is produced. The only remedy and safety is that we shall stand by the Constitution as our fathers made it, obey the laws as they are passed, while they stand the proper test, and sustain the decisions of the Supreme Court and the constituted authorities.